THE *Simpleness* *of the* WAY

THE *Simpleness* of the WAY

❧

DANIEL K JUDD

BOOKCRAFT
SALT LAKE CITY, UTAH

Library of Congress Catalog Card Number 97-77973
ISBN 1-57008-399-1

First Printing, 1998

Printed in the United States of America

"[The Lord] sent fiery flying serpents among them; and after they were bitten he prepared a way that they might be healed; and the labor which they had to perform was to look; and because of the simpleness of the way, or the easiness of it, there were many who perished."

—1 Nephi 17:41

CONTENTS

ACKNOWLEDGMENTS

Many friends, colleagues, and family members have made this book possible. I am grateful for those who have been willing to share so much of their lives with me. Richard L. Judd, Valton E. Jackson, Frank M. Bradshaw, Elder Hartman Rector Jr., Jerry A. Wilson, and Richard N. Williams have taught me, each in a different way, the power of the restored gospel.

I am especially indebted to my colleague, C. Terry Warner, professor of philosophy at Brigham Young University. Brother Warner's work on conscience and sin (see chapters two and six) has not only provided me an intellectual framework for understanding these issues, but has also helped me in my understanding of the scriptures and related statements of the leaders of the Church. Though I am grateful for his influence, Brother Warner is not responsible for the use I have made of his material.

Special thanks to my research assistants, Aimee Strong and Amy Osmond, who reviewed various parts of the manuscript and offered important suggestions. Cory H. Maxwell and Janna Lee Nielsen of Bookcraft have also been a great help in the preparation of the manuscript.

I am grateful to my father, LeRoy P. Judd, for teaching me how to work and to my mother, Phyllis Farnsworth Judd, for teaching me about what it really means to be a Christian.

Thanks also to my brothers, Dennis, Richard, and Barry, for their support and love.

My children, Jacob, Jessica, Rachel, and Adam, have played a large part in the writing of this book. Not only have they provided inspiration and material for several of the stories in this book, they have provided a wealth of love and good humor as well.

Finally, I am eternally indebted to my wife, Kaye Seegmiller Judd. Without her love, conversation, support, and technical expertise, this book would not have been written.

While I have endeavored to be true to the words of prophets, both ancient and modern, this book represents my interpretation of what they have taught. This publication is my own endeavor and is not intended to officially represent Brigham Young University or The Church of Jesus Christ of Latter-day Saints. Please look beyond my limitations and learn of the great plan of the Eternal God and the everlasting hope that is contained in "the simpleness of the way" (1 Nephi 17:41).

INTRODUCTION

We are greatly blessed to live at a time when the gospel of Jesus Christ has been restored to the earth in its fulness. These latter days have been described by President Gordon B. Hinckley as "the greatest season in the history of the Church."[1] But we must also acknowledge that while we live in a golden age of the history of the Church, not all is well in Zion nor in the world in general. There are many individuals, marriages, and families, within and without the Church, who are experiencing serious problems. From the *Wall Street Journal* we read that from 1960 to the present there has been a "560% increase in violent crime; a 419% increase in illegitimate births; a quadrupling in divorce rates; a tripling of the percentage of children living in single-parent homes; [and] more than a 200% increase in the teenage suicide rate."[2] While these statistics report what has happened in the United States these past few decades, they are representative of what is happening throughout the world.

The Apostle Paul prophesied of our day when he wrote: "This know also, that in the last days perilous times shall come. For men shall be lovers of their own selves, covetous, boasters, proud, blasphemers, disobedient to parents, unthankful, unholy, without natural affection, trucebreakers, false accusers, incontinent, fierce, despisers of those that are good, traitors, heady, highminded, lovers of pleasures more than lovers of God; having a form of godliness, but denying the power thereof. . . . [They shall be] ever learning, and never able to come to the knowledge of the truth." (2 Timothy 3:1–5, 7.) President Boyd K. Packer stated in 1995 that "the prophets and Apostles know full well that the perilous times Paul prophesied for the last days are now upon us."[3]

Many wonder to whom they should turn when confronted with difficult personal, marital, and family problems. They ask, in the words of one of our latter-day hymns:

> Where can I turn for peace? Where is my solace
> When other sources cease to make me whole? . . .
> Where, in my need to know, where can I run?[4]

Answering these questions is crucial to our happiness. Not only will the ways we respond to the challenges of life influence our happiness in this life, but our very salvation may be in the balance as well.

Some would say the answers to the problems of our day are to be found in the disciplines of psychiatry, psychology, genetic engineering, or in educational reform. Others argue for more specific changes in economic strategy, political leadership, or gender equality. Still others have lost all hope of there even being meaningful answers to the problems we face. Proposed solutions to the challenges of life are nearly as numerous as those who propose them.

As members of The Church of Jesus Christ of Latter-day Saints, we have been counseled to turn to our Heavenly Father, to the scriptures, and to the words of our living prophets for guidance. But some ask, "Is the gospel a sufficient source of truth to address the complex problems of our day?" The pages that follow attempt to explore some of the problems we face and to consider some of the answers to these problems from a gospel perspective.

The Great Plan of the Eternal God

When I was first called to serve as a bishop I was humbled but felt as well prepared as any new bishop could. I had professional training as a psychologist, I had taught in the Church Educational System for a number of years, I had fulfilled a mission, and I had served in a bishopric and in numerous other Church callings. I was confident and enthused about this new opportunity to serve, but little did I realize the enormity of the challenges that lay ahead. It took only a few days to learn that serving as a bishop was much more difficult than I had envisioned; I wasn't nearly as well prepared as I had naively believed. Like Moses, I learned that "man is nothing, which thing I never had supposed" (Moses 1:10). I was overwhelmed by the many difficult and sobering situations with which I was regularly confronted. In addition to the constant administrative details that come with leadership, I found the wide variety of my ward members' personal, marital, and family problems especially challenging.

One evening a ward member called on the telephone and informed me that he and his wife had decided to file for divorce. Even though I had previously spent many hours with them, I asked if I could meet with them once again before they carried out their decision. They were hesitant, but each of them reluctantly agreed to an appointment. As I began to contemplate how I would approach this discussion, I began to sense that while I had given this couple competent counsel, mostly based on my professional training, I hadn't represented the Lord as I felt a faithful bishop should.

In the period between Brother Carter's* call announcing his and his wife's decision to divorce and the time I was to meet with them, I began to study and pray with an intensity

---

* The "Carters" (not their real name) have graciously granted me permission to relate our story.

that I had rarely experienced before. A few days later, as I was preparing to teach religion class, I read a conference address by President Ezra Taft Benson that I found to be instructive and enlightening. President Benson stated:

> We need to use the everlasting word to awaken those in deep sleep so they will awake "unto God" [Alma 5:7].
>
> I am deeply concerned about what we are doing to teach the Saints at all levels the gospel of Jesus Christ as completely and authoritatively as do the Book of Mormon and the Doctrine and Covenants. By this I mean teaching the "great plan of the Eternal God," to use the words of Amulek (Alma 34:9).
>
> Are we using the messages and the method of teaching found in the Book of Mormon and other scriptures of the Restoration to teach this great plan of the Eternal God? . . .
>
> Brethren and sisters, we all need to take a careful inventory of our performance and also the performance of those over whom we preside to be sure that we are teaching the "great plan of the Eternal God" to the Saints.[5]

I had read Amulek's and President Benson's words before, but this time the words "the great plan of the Eternal God" stood out. As I pondered these words I was intrigued with the idea that while I had spent several years learning the plans, theories, therapies, and philosophies that had been devised by men, perhaps I had not taken as seriously as I could the plan God himself had established to bless and redeem his children.

As I searched the scriptures, I found that the Lord's plan has been described in different ways: "the merciful plan of the great Creator" (2 Nephi 9:6), "the plan of our God" (2 Nephi 9:13), "the great and eternal plan of deliverance from death" (2 Nephi 11:5), "the great plan of redemption" (Jacob 6:8), "the plan of salvation" (Jarom 1:2), "the plan of redemption" (Alma 12:25), "the great plan of the Eternal God" (Alma 34:9), "the great and eternal plan of redemption" (Alma 34:16), "the great plan of happiness" (Alma 42:8), and "the great plan of mercy" (Alma 42:31).

As I continued to study the Book of Mormon, together with the writings and lectures of President Benson and others,[6] I learned that the "great plan of the Eternal God" was founded on the doctrines of the Creation, the Fall, and the atonement of Jesus Christ. Elder Bruce R. McConkie described these doctrines as the "three pillars of eternity."[7] The more I studied, the more clearly I could see that this plan was more profound than I had ever realized.

As the next few days approached and passed, I also came to realize that I had not been teaching and counseling the Carters in the manner the Lord would have me. I could now see that instead of helping them to understand their differences, assisting them to communicate more effectively, and facilitating some sort of compromise, I was responsible and privileged to teach this troubled couple to come unto Christ through the "great plan of the Eternal God"!

While it wasn't yet clear to me how I could help the Carters make direct application of the Lord's plan, I sensed that if I could begin by helping them understand the doctrines of the Creation, the Fall, and the Atonement, these doctrines could become a meaningful part of helping them heal their troubled relationship. As I thought about what I was learning, I began to feel a growing eagerness to meet with them and share what I felt the Lord would have them know.

The time for my appointment with Brother and Sister Carter arrived. After offering a prayer, I asked Brother Carter if he could remember the first time he and his wife met. His response was, "Bishop, why are you asking me to talk about the *beginning* of our relationship when we have come to talk about the *end?*" After some persuasion, Brother Carter began to reconstruct the events and describe his feelings about his and his wife's initial dating, courtship, and early days of marriage. His description startled me; without even realizing it, in recounting the beginning of his relationship with his wife, he was describing the first phase of the Lord's plan for their relationship—the creation. I was beginning to understand how we should proceed.

While not agreeing on the specifics of their initial meeting, Brother and Sister Carter acknowledged that their first few months of dating and courtship had been a Garden-of-Eden-like existence. They were secure in one another's love and had shared a great hope for the future. In a metaphorical sense, their sun was shining, their grass was green, their water clear, and their sky blue.

What this couple had experienced in their first few months of marriage is typical of many relationships, not only in marriage but in other aspects of life as well. Many of us can recall the feelings of excitement and hope we experienced as we first made the team; received a mission call or letter of acceptance; made or accepted a marriage proposal; experienced pregnancy and childbirth, graduation, promotion, retirement; or anticipated the beginning of any new opportunity. I was going through this same process personally in having moved to a new area, my wife having a new baby, and serving as a new bishop. While the process of creation is important to any new experience or relationship, the real test of life comes in the part of the Lord's plan that follows—opposition through the fall.

As Brother Carter continued to describe the first few weeks and months of his and Sister Carter's relationship, he began to cry and then to weep. He later described how devastating it was for him to be confronted with the incongruity of his feelings for his wife, for what had once been so beautiful was turning to ashes. Also to my surprise, as Brother Carter wept, Sister Carter reached over, put her arm around him, and said, "It's going to be okay, honey." I had previously heard her describe him in a variety of ways, but never "honey." It appeared as if we were making progress.

Later in our conversation, I mentioned the hope I had felt when Sister Carter had used such an endearing term as *honey* in her attempt to comfort her husband. She responded by emphatically insisting that she hadn't, and it was sobering to observe how quickly a conversation can fall from a state of *creation* to one of *opposition*. Even though our conversation was at times strained, difficult, and confrontational, I was at peace with what we were doing, for this time I had confidence we were addressing Brother and Sister Carter's problems the right way.

As our conversation continued, I learned that this couple's understanding of the doctrines of the gospel was very limited. Even though they had been members of the Church all of their lives, they had naively believed that if the Lord would have them be together, and if they kept the commandments, life would proceed smoothly without serious challenge. I reviewed with them the doctrine of the Fall as contained in the Book of Mormon. The Prophet Lehi taught his son Jacob that the fall of Adam and Eve, and the opposition each of us faces, was and is both necessary and essential to the Lord's plan: "For it must needs be, that there is an *opposition in all things.* If not so, my first-born in the wilderness, righteousness could not be brought to pass, neither wickedness, neither holiness nor misery, neither good nor bad. Wherefore, all things must needs be a compound in one; wherefore, if it should be one body it must needs remain as dead, having no life neither death, nor corruption nor incorruption, happiness nor misery, neither sense nor insensibility." (2 Nephi 2:11; emphasis added.)

As we discussed the essential role of Christ and the Atonement, it became clear to me that the Carters weren't so much rejecting the Savior as they were ignorant of the truths he taught. Like many of us, they knew of Christ and wanted to have faith in him, but they didn't really understand how. After our initial session, discussing the creation and fall of their relationship, we spent the next several appointments discussing the meaning and healing power of the atonement of Jesus Christ. It was meaningful for them, and for me, to realize that the central purpose of the Atonement is reconciliation. Just as each of us may be reconciled with our Father in Heaven through the sacrifice of his Son, so also may we be reconciled one to another. The Apostle Paul taught, "For if, when we were enemies, we were reconciled to God by the death of his Son, much more, being reconciled, we shall be saved by his life" (Romans 5:10). Not only does the suffering and death of Jesus Christ enable us to be cleansed from sin and strengthened through adversity (see Alma 7:11–12), the Savior's life and teachings serve as the perfect example for each of us to follow.

It was miraculous to watch this couple's hope for their marriage grow as their faith in Christ increased. The Savior taught, "If ye will have faith in me ye shall have power to do whatsoever thing is expedient in me" (Moroni 7:33). The Prophet Moroni added, "Wherefore, if a man have faith he must needs have hope; for without faith there cannot be any hope" (Moroni 7:42). We must begin by having faith in Christ if there is to be any hope of experiencing the joy that endures longer than a season (see 3 Nephi 27:11).

During the weeks and months that followed, this particular couple and I were blessed with many insights relative to their problems and the solutions to those problems in light of the doctrines of the Creation, the Fall, and the Atonement. This couple, and many others like them, continue to labor and at times are heavy laden, but are learning to "come unto Christ, and partake of the goodness of God" (Jacob 1:7). We can have hope, for we have a plan, even "the great plan of the Eternal God" (Alma 34:9).

The Simpleness of the Way

The title for this book, *The Simpleness of the Way*, is a reminder that while the challenges and questions of life are often complex, the elegant truths of the gospel of Jesus Christ have a way of simplifying the solutions we seek. President Howard W. Hunter once wrote: "In this world of confusion and rushing, temporal progress, we need to return to the simplicity of Christ. We need to love, honor, and worship him. To acquire spirituality and have its influence in our lives, we cannot become confused and misdirected by the twisted teachings of the modernist. We need to study the simple fundamentals of the truths taught by the Master and eliminate the controversial."[8]

In one of the prophet Nephi's discourses, he provides additional details of the biblical account of the children of Israel being bitten by "fiery serpents" (Numbers 21:6) as they journeyed in the wilderness. From Nephi's account we learn that many of those stricken by the bites of the serpents died because they didn't exercise faith in the simple solution provided by the Lord. Nephi described the events as follows: "He [the Lord] sent fiery flying serpents among them; and after they were bitten he prepared a way that they might be healed; and the labor which they had to perform was to look; and because of the *simpleness of the way,* or the easiness of it, there were many who perished" (1 Nephi 17:41; emphasis added).

In order for them to be healed, all that was required of those who were afflicted was to look upon the brass serpent the prophet Moses had placed upon a pole. Both the Book of Mormon and the Bible (see John 3:14–15) tell us that the serpent was a symbol of Jesus Christ and that healing can be realized by coming unto him. The prophet Alma taught the Zoramites: "Behold, he [Christ] was spoken of by Moses; yea, and behold a type was raised up in the wilderness [the brazen serpent], that whosoever would look upon it might live. And many did look and live." (Alma 33:19.) Alma further explained that a few of the Israelites believed the words of Moses, but the majority, because of the hardness of their hearts, did not believe that looking at the serpent—looking to Christ—could heal them. "But few understood the meaning of those things, and this because of the hardness of their hearts. But there were many who were so hardened that they would not look, therefore they perished. Now the reason they would not look is because *they did not believe that it would heal them.*" (Alma 33:20; emphasis added.)

Alma continued his message with a promise to the Zoramites of healing for the obedient and of prolonged suffering and destruction for those who chose not to believe:

> O my brethren, if ye could be healed by merely casting about your eyes *that ye might be healed,* would ye not behold quickly, or would ye rather harden your hearts in unbelief, and be slothful, that ye would not cast about your eyes, that ye might perish?

If so, wo shall come upon you; but if not so, then cast about your eyes and begin to believe in the Son of God, that he will come to redeem his people, and that he shall suffer and die to atone for their sins; and that he shall rise again from the dead, which shall bring to pass the resurrection, that all men shall stand before him, to be judged at the last and judgment day, according to their works. (Alma 33:21–22; emphasis added.)

Alma finished his discourse by promising the Zoramites that if they would take Christ and his gospel seriously, their burdens would be lightened: "And now, my brethren, I desire that ye shall plant this word in your hearts, and as it beginneth to swell even so nourish it by your faith. And behold, it will become a tree, springing up in you unto everlasting life. And then may God grant unto you that your burdens may be light, through the joy of his Son. And even all this can ye do if ye will. Amen." (Alma 33:23.)

What of the Saints of the latter days—do we believe that Christ can heal us of our fiery infirmities, or have we become as the unbelieving Israelites of old? Just as Moses, Alma, and other prophets taught their people of the healing power of Christ and his atonement, latter-day prophets have given similar invitations in our day. President Howard W. Hunter once stated: "Please remember this one thing. If our lives and our faith are centered upon Jesus Christ and his restored gospel, nothing can ever go permanently wrong. On the other hand, if our lives are not centered on the Savior and his teachings, no other success can ever be permanently right."[9]

What about those of us who are experiencing serious emotional problems or who are in unhappy marriages? What meaning does Jesus Christ and his gospel have for us in what we are doing to solve our problems? President Hunter also reminded us that "this world needs the gospel of Jesus Christ as restored through the Prophet Joseph Smith. The gospel provides the *only way* the world will ever know peace."[10] President Hinckley has stated: "The answer to our problems lies in following the simple gospel of Jesus Christ, the Son of God, who brought into the world His Father's love."[11]

While prophets, both ancient and modern, have written of the blessings of living the gospel of Christ, they have also warned us of the consequences of unbelief. "And the whole world lieth in sin, and groaneth under darkness and under the bondage of sin . . . *because they come not unto me.* For whoso cometh not unto me is under the bondage of sin. . . . And your minds in times past have been darkened because of unbelief, and because you have treated lightly the things you have received—*which vanity and unbelief have brought the whole church under condemnation.*" (D&C 84:49–50, 54–55; emphasis added.)

The scriptures plainly teach that the primary reason for many of the problems we face in the world, and especially in the Church, is that we have rejected the message of the Book of Mormon by failing to come unto Christ. The Lord warns us that this condemnation rests upon us all and will continue until we repent and begin to take Christ and his message more seriously. "And this condemnation resteth upon the children of Zion, *even all.* And they shall remain under this condemnation *until* they repent and remember the new covenant, even the Book of Mormon and the former commandments which I have given them, not only to say, but to do according to that which I have written—that they may bring forth fruit meet for their Father's kingdom; otherwise there remaineth a scourge and judgment to be poured out upon the children of Zion." (D&C 84:56–58; emphasis added.)

It is a mistake to think that those whom the Lord describes as being under "condemnation" are only the "less active" members of the Church or even those who have outright rejected the gospel message. The Lord plainly states that "this condemnation resteth upon the children of Zion, *even all.*"

When I raise the question to my students at Brigham Young University, "What is the condemnation that we as members of the Church are under?" the majority will answer with certainty, "We haven't been reading the Book of Mormon."

While this answer is certainly correct, I sometimes wonder if we really understand what it means to take the Book of Mormon as seriously as we should. Inasmuch as the purpose of the Book of Mormon is the "convincing of the Jew and Gentile that Jesus is the Christ,"[12] could the condemnation be that we aren't claiming the blessings available to us by faithfully following the example of Jesus Christ through a covenant relationship with our Heavenly Father? My intention in writing this book is to help each of us evaluate our own lives and come to an understanding of what it means and what we can do to more fully "come unto Christ, and be perfected in him" (Moroni 10:32).

Following the outline provided by "the great plan of happiness" (Alma 42:8), I have divided this book into three sections: (1) the Creation, (2) the Fall, and (3) the Atonement. In each section, I have attempted to address specific issues relevant to each doctrine. I have also attempted to "liken all scriptures unto us" (1 Nephi 19:23) by providing numerous examples of the significance of these doctrines in the lives of individuals, marriages, and families who are facing the challenges of life.

NOTES

1. "President Hinckley Completes 8-day Tour," *Church News*, 25 May 1997, p. 10.

2. William J. Bennett, "Quantifying America's Decline," *Wall Street Journal*, March 15, 1993; as cited by Gordon B. Hinckley, "Bring Up a Child in the Way He Should Go," *Ensign*, November 1993, p. 59.

3. Boyd K. Packer, "The Shield of Faith," *Ensign*, May 1995, p. 8.

4. Emma Lou Thayne and Joleen G. Meredith, "Where Can I Turn for Peace," *Hymns*, no. 129.

5. Ezra Taft Benson, "The Book of Mormon and the Doctrine and Covenants," *Ensign*, May 1987, pp. 84–85.

6. Jerry A. Wilson, my former Church Educational System area director, was the first to share with me the significance of what President Benson was teaching. I am indebted to Brother Wilson's tutelage and friendship.

7. Bruce R. McConkie, *A New Witness for the Articles of Faith* (Salt Lake City: Deseret Book Co., 1985), p. 81.

8. Howard W. Hunter, "Where, Then, Is Hope," *Improvement Era,* December 1970, p. 117.

9. Howard W. Hunter, " 'Fear Not, Little Flock,' " *Brigham Young University 1988–89 Devotional and Fireside Speeches* (Provo: University Publications, 1989), p. 112.

10. Howard W. Hunter, "Come to the God of All Truth," *Ensign,* September 1994, p. 72; emphasis added.

11. Gordon B. Hinckley, "Some Lessons I Learned as a Boy," *Ensign,* May 1993, p. 59.

12. Book of Mormon, title page.

SECTION ONE

The Creation

❧

1

And I, God, created man in mine own image,
in the image of mine Only Begotten created I him;
male and female created I them.
—Moses 2:27

THE DIVINE ORIGIN AND
POTENTIAL OF MAN

At first glance, one may wonder how the doctrine of creation, introduced thousands of years ago, can in any way relate to the solving of our present problems, but the answer is really quite simple. One of the basic reasons for the detailed manner in which the Creation is outlined in the scriptures is to teach the divine origin and potential of man. In the Pearl of Great Price we read, "And I, God, created man *in mine own image,* in the image of mine Only Begotten created I him; male and female created I them (Moses 2:27; emphasis added). This verse follows a detailed account of how each form of animal and plant life was created "after their kind" (see Moses 2:11–12, 21, 24–25). One of the truths which can be understood from this sequence of verses is that Adam and Eve were not simply the evolutionary products of lesser life forms. Neither were they mystically created ex nihilo (out of nothing), as some would have us believe. Knowledge of our divine parentage illuminates our own heritage and potential as well. We are not merely a higher order of animal with the accompanying animalistic appetites, drives, and patterns of behavior. Prophets, both ancient and modern, have taught us that we are sons and daughters of God in the process of developing his same "character, perfections, and attributes."[1]

17

The First Presidency taught: "Man is the child of God, formed in the divine image and endowed with divine attributes, and even as the infant son of an earthly father and mother is capable in due time of becoming a man, so the undeveloped offspring of celestial parentage is capable, by experience through ages and aeons, of evolving into a God."[2]

On occasion my students at Brigham Young University will ask, "Has the Church ever given an official position on evolution?" The answer is yes and no. Evolution in general? No. The origin of man? Yes! In November of 1909 (the centennial anniversary of Charles Darwin's birth), the First Presidency of the Church (Joseph F. Smith, John R. Winder, and Anthon H. Lund) issued the following statement, which they described as "the position held by the Church" concerning the origin of man. In part, the message reads as follows:

> It is held by some that Adam was not the first man upon this earth, and that the original human being was a development from lower orders of the animal creation. These, however, are the theories of men. The word of the Lord declares that Adam was "the first man of all men" (Moses 1:34), and we are therefore in duty bound to regard him as the primal parent of our race. It was shown to the brother of Jared that all men were created in the beginning after the image of God; and whether we take this to mean the spirit or the body, or both, it commits us to the same conclusion: Man began life as a human being, in the likeness of our heavenly Father.
>
> True it is that the body of man enters upon its career as a tiny germ or embryo, which becomes an infant, quickened at a certain stage by the spirit whose tabernacle it is, and the child, after being born, develops into a man. There is nothing in this, however, to indicate that the original man, the first of our race, began life as anything less than a man, or less than the human germ or embryo that becomes a man.
>
> Man, by searching, cannot find out God. Never, unaided, will he discover the truth about the beginning of human life. The Lord must reveal Himself, or remain unrevealed; and the same is true of the facts relating to the origin of Adam's race—

God alone can reveal them. Some of these facts, however, are already known, and what has been made known it is our duty to receive and retain.

The Church of Jesus Christ of Latter-day Saints, basing its belief on divine revelation, ancient and modern, proclaims man to be the direct and lineal offspring of Deity. God himself is an exalted man, perfected, enthroned, and supreme. By His almighty power He organized the earth, and all that it contains, from spirit and element, which exist co-eternally with Himself. He formed every plant that grows, and every animal that breathes, each after its own kind, spiritually and temporally—"that which is spiritual being in the likeness of that which is temporal, and that which is temporal in the likeness of that which is spiritual." He made the tadpole and the ape, the lion and the elephant but He did not make them in His own image, nor endow them with Godlike reason and intelligence. Nevertheless, the whole animal creation will be perfected and perpetuated in the Hereafter, each class in its "distinct order or sphere," and will enjoy "eternal felicity." That fact has been made plain in this dispensation. (Doctrine & Covenants 77:3.)[3]

While there is much controversy over the specifics of the theory of evolution, the First Presidency has been very clear concerning the points of doctrine that (1) life did not come about by "chance" and (2) that man *did not* ascend from lesser forms of life.

Elder Boyd K. Packer, of the Quorum of the Twelve Apostles, speaking at a Book of Mormon symposium at Brigham Young University, outlined the implications of believing otherwise:

The comprehension of man as no more than a specialized animal cannot help but affect how one behaves. A conviction that man did evolve from animals *fosters the mentality that man is not responsible for moral conduct.* Animals are controlled to a very large extent by physical urges. Promiscuity is a common pattern in the reproduction of animals. In many subtle ways, the perception that man is an animal and likewise controlled by urges invites that kind of behavior so apparent in society today. A self-image in which we regard ourselves as children of God sponsors one kind of behavior. A conclusion which equates man to animals fosters another kind of behavior entirely. Consequences which spring from that single false premise account for much of what society now suffers.[4]

Even though the theory of man's evolutionary development wasn't formally introduced until the nineteenth century, Book of Mormon prophets warned of its evil influence years before. The anti-Christ Korihor taught what some evolutionists have called the "survival of the fittest" when he told the people of Ammon that "every man fared in this life according to the management of the creature; therefore every man prospered according to his genius, and that every man conquered according to his strength" (Alma 30:17). As with most false philosophies, there are some elements of truth to the ideas Korihor taught. Personal management, genius, and strength do play a role in man's success, but the problem is found in the fact that what Korihor was teaching is atheistic. He made no allowance for the reality of the influence of God. Korihor's doctrines also represent a preoccupation with his own success and not a desire to bless the lives of others. This same godless preoccupation with self is found in much of the "self-help" literature that fills many bookstores.

Korihor connected his selfish, atheistic philosophy with a related idea that has come to be called "moral relativism."* Korihor displayed his relativistic position by believing that "whatsoever a man did was no crime" (Alma 30:17). The prophet Lehi warned of the consequences of moral relativism in the following: "And if ye shall say there is no law, ye shall also say there is no sin. If ye shall say there is no sin, ye shall also say there is no righteousness. And if there be no righteousness

---

* The philosophy of relativism rejects the existence of absolute truth and accepts the idea that man is free to create what is right and wrong based on his own desires.

there be no happiness. And if there be no righteousness nor happiness there be no punishment nor misery. And if these things are not there is no God. And if there is no God we are not, neither the earth; for there could have been no creation of things, neither to act nor to be acted upon; wherefore, all things must have vanished away." (2 Nephi 2:13.)

To believe that man evolved from lesser forms of life is to believe that man is simply a higher form of animal and is not by nature a moral being. This philosophy invites the idea that morality (right and wrong) is man-made and is subject to change depending on circumstance. Without absolute law, a belief in an absolute Lawgiver becomes suspect, and people are left with the idea that right and wrong do not exist. Without the understanding of our relationship to heavenly parents, we are left with the anxiety that we are completely alone in the world and subject to the manipulations of forces beyond our control.

Gratefully, we are not alone. God is literally our Father and wants us to have happy and meaningful lives. He also knows that for us to have a fulness of joy we must eventually become like him by living as he lives. Our Heavenly Father wants us to understand that the same attributes he possesses can be ours as well. Lorenzo Snow taught, "As man now is, God once was: as God now is, man may be."[5] Man's divine origin and potential are the fundamental messages of the doctrine of creation.

One way of coming to comprehend our divine identity is to study the character of God. As we come to comprehend the character of God, we also come to comprehend who we really are, for we are literally his children. The Prophet Joseph Smith taught that "if men do not comprehend the character of God, they do not comprehend themselves."[6] Thus, by coming to comprehend the character of God we can come to understand our true identities as his children and our potential to become like him. Coming to know our relationship to God can also help us be better able to face the challenges of life. The following story, written by a friend of mine, illustrates how important this understanding can be:

As I was growing up, I belonged to what some people might call a model family. I had kind, loving parents with strong, moral beliefs. As a family we did all those things that healthy families did. We attended Church meetings as well as working in and supporting the various auxiliaries of [the] Church. We worked in our community. We supported our schools. My mother was strong, independent, and loving. My father was supportive and patient. Though my parents had grown up in homes filled with anger, mistrust, abuse, and alcoholism, they were overcoming the past. I felt safe.

In my teen years our family began to fall apart. I learned that my father had violated many of the truths he had taught me to hold sacred. Many sad and terrible things happened to my family during this time, and the world that I had known as a child began to fall apart.

With my family shattered and my father's indiscretions exposed, we all split up. If not physically, emotionally. And spiritually we gave up. We all left the Church we had always known.

I struggled on for several years, trying to help my family in the long, painful healing process. Most of the time I felt empty and lost. During this time I met and married my husband. I was searching for that security and peace I had known as a child. But life was anything but happy and peaceful for us.

Then one day, quite by accident, I ran into some members of the Church. And in talking and visiting with them I realized what my life needed to get back on track. So, I began my journey back, even knowing that I was putting my marriage at risk. I began praying to my Heavenly Father, asking for strength, praying for answers. I also returned to the scriptures. Studying and pondering. At times I felt I was getting stronger, beginning to feel that peace of childhood.

But something was missing. I had always looked to my parents for the confirmation of truths. Now that support was gone. My mother was struggling with her own pain, and my father was exposed as a hypocrite. But I had in time, come to realize that the weaknesses were in my father, not in these sacred truths.

Now I was struggling with my own weaknesses. In trying to live a Christlike life, I many times would stumble. I would feel like giving up. "After all," I would say to myself, "I am my father's daughter. Why should I keep trying? The apple never does fall far from the tree." Many times I have almost given up. I would look at my own children, their innocent yet strong spirits, and wonder again about the apple and that tree. In my studies of the scriptures, I gained new testimony of repentance and the atonement of Jesus Christ. I realized that all sin had already been atoned for. I didn't have to pay for the sins of my father. I did not need to punish myself for his weaknesses. All of these realizations helped, but still at my own times of weakness I would catch myself saying, "You're just like your father!"

This struggle went on, back and forth, until I allowed myself to realize that I have more heavenly roots. I do have physical parents, but I also have spiritual parents—a Heavenly Father and Mother. This revelation of something I had known all my life gave me the peace and security I had been searching for. I have heavenly parents who love me, who guide and direct me. I have a brother, Jesus Christ, who loved me enough that he gave his life for me. With this kind of family tree, how could I quit? The apple doesn't fall very far from the tree. I just had to learn from which tree I came. There are times when I still feel doubt creeping in, times when I allow myself to despair. But at these times, now, I hear myself saying, "Chin up—after all you are your Father's daughter. Your Heavenly Father's daughter."[7]

Coming to understand the literalness of this woman's relationship with her Heavenly Father and her divine potential helped her to be free of the sins of her earthly father (see 1 Kings 15:3). She came to understand that her divine potential far exceeded the influence of her genetic inheritance. Elder Dallin H. Oaks, of the Quorum of Twelve Apostles, has said:

Latter-day Saints should be constantly concerned with teaching and emphasizing those great and powerful eternal truths

that will help us find our way back to the presence of our
Heavenly Father. . . .

Consider the power of the idea taught in our beloved song
"I Am a Child of God" (*Hymns*, 1985, no. 301). . . . Here is
the answer to one of life's great questions, "Who am I?" I am
a child of God with a spirit lineage to heavenly parents. That
parentage defines our eternal potential. That powerful idea is a
potent antidepressant. It can strengthen each of us to make
righteous choices and to seek the best that is within us.[8]

While our prophets, both ancient and modern, have revealed many important things relative to the origin of man,
many questions remained unanswered. This ambiguity, though
difficult to deal with, is also an integral part of the Lord's plan.
Elder Boyd K. Packer has taught: "All things not only *are not*
known but *must not* be so convincingly clear as to eliminate the
need for faith. That would nullify agency and defeat the purpose of the plan of salvation. Tests of faith are growing experiences. . . . It is my conviction that a full knowledge of the origin of man must await further discovery, further revelation."[9]

As we come to understand our divine parentage and strive
to fulfill our divine potential, we can experience the joy, peace,
and hope promised us by our Heavenly Father, for we are literally his children (see Romans 15:13).

NOTES

1. "Lecture Third," *Lectures on Faith* (Salt Lake City: Deseret Book
Co., 1985), pp. 38–48.

2. Joseph F. Smith, John R. Winder, and Anthon H. Lund, in James
R. Clark, comp., *Messages of the First Presidency of The Church of Jesus
Christ of Latter-day Saints,* 6 vols. (Salt Lake City: Bookcraft, 1965–75),
4:206.

3. Ibid., 4:205–6.

4. Boyd K. Packer, "The Law and the Light," *The Book of Mormon:
Jacob Through Words of Mormon, to Learn with Joy,* ed. Monte Nyman

and Charles Tate, Jr. (Provo: Religious Studies Center, Brigham Young University, 1990), pp. 6–7.

5. Eliza R. Snow Smith, *Biography and Family Record of Lorenzo Snow* (Salt Lake City: Deseret News Company Printers, 1884), p. 46.

6. Joseph Smith, *Teachings of the Prophet Joseph Smith,* comp. Joseph Fielding Smith (Salt Lake City: Deseret Book Co., 1938), p. 343.

7. Used with permission from the author.

8. Dallin H. Oaks, "Powerful Ideas," *Ensign,* November 1995, p. 25.

9. Boyd K. Packer, "The Law and the Light," p. 8.

2

Our conscience might be described as a memory,
a residual awareness of who we really are,
of our true identity.
—Boyd K. Packer

CONSCIENCE: A SOURCE OF
OUR DIVINE IDENTITY

One of the ways we first come to know Jesus Christ, perceive the will of our Father in Heaven, and begin to understand our divine parentage and potential, is through our conscience. Elder Boyd K. Packer has written:

> *Conscience* is a most interesting word. It is made up of the prefix *con,* meaning "with," and the word *science,* meaning "to know." The *Oxford English Dictionary* says it comes from the Latin *conscientia,* meaning "knowledge [knowing] within oneself." The first definition listed there is "inward knowl-

---

My treatment of conscience in this chapter is based on the work of C. Terry Warner, professor of philosophy at Brigham Young University. His profound insights concerning conscience and sin have provided me the intellectual framework for understanding the workings of conscience (including its very nature), what happens when we fail to heed its promptings, and how our experience of conscience, of ourselves, and of others changes when we fail to follow what we feel to be right. See Professor Warner's, *Bonds of Anguish, Bond of Love,* available from the Arbinger Company, 350 West Broadway, Salt Lake City, Utah 84101. See also, *C. Terry Warner: Oxford Papers,* ed. Duane Boyce (Salt Lake City: Arbinger Press, 1997).

edge, consciousness, inmost thought, mind." The second one is "consciousness of right and wrong," or in just two words, "moral sense."

Our conscience might be described as a memory, a residual awareness of who we really are, of our true identity. It is perhaps the best example of the fact that we can become aware of truths because we feel them rather than by knowing them because we perceive them through the physical senses.[1]

It is through our conscience, or Spirit of Christ as it is called in the Book of Mormon, that our Heavenly Father first illuminates the path on which we must trod to claim the blessings of Christ and the Atonement. The Prophet Mormon has written the following concerning the Spirit of Christ: "For behold, the Spirit of Christ is given to every man, that he may know good from evil; wherefore, I show unto you the way to judge; for every thing which inviteth to do good, and to persuade to believe in Christ, is sent forth by the power and gift of Christ; wherefore ye may know with a perfect knowledge it is of God" (Moroni 7:16).

Our conscience, or "light of Christ" (Moroni 7:18), can be experienced in different ways. If we are living truthfully (consistent with the light and truth that is available to us), we will typically experience our conscience as a gentle invitation. We may even reach a point of selflessness, where we aren't even aware that we are being prompted or acting upon a prompting (see 3 Nephi 9:20).

If we are not living truthfully (not doing what we know to be right), we will experience our conscience as demanding and irritating, always giving us something we have to do. Being true to what we know to be right will eventually lead us to peace and greater understanding, while not being true is always the beginning of greater problems to follow.[2]

The scriptures teach us that our consciences (the light of Christ) aren't simply manifestations of the expectations of our culture. Our moral nature (as manifested through our conscience) is a fundamental part of what it means to be a son or daughter of God. The Apostle Paul taught that conscience transcends religious and cultural training: "For when the Gentiles, which have not the law, do by nature the things contained in the law, these, having not the law, are a law unto themselves: which shew the work of the law written in their hearts, their conscience also bearing witness, and their thoughts the mean while accusing or else excusing one another" (Romans 2:14–15).

If we believe our conscience to simply be the product of environmental influences, questions of right and wrong become relative to personal opinion and circumstance and the topic of constant debate. On the other hand, believing an omniscient God to be the source of absolute truth, gives us the confidence and ability to exercise faith in his guidance. The Prophet Joseph Smith taught: "Without the knowledge of all things God would not be able to save any portion of his creatures; for it is by reason of the knowledge which he has of all things, from the beginning to the end, that enables him to give that understanding to his creatures by which they are made partakers of eternal life; and if it were not for the idea existing in the minds of men that God had all knowledge it would be impossible for them to exercise faith in him."[3]

Being able to discern the differences between the revelations of God through our conscience and the distorted expectations of ourselves or others is critical, for one leads to eventual peace and the other to misery. While many of us go against the light we have been given by not doing those things we know are right, others of us confuse conscience with societal expectations and get lost in the artificial light of perfectionism. Consider the following story of Esther, a faithful Latter-day Saint striving to live up to a counterfeited sense of right and wrong:

> Esther was trying to be the perfect wife and mother. Every morning she woke up announcing to herself: "This is the day I will be perfect. The house will be organized, I will not yell at my children, and I will finish everything important I have planned." Every night she went to bed discouraged, because

she had failed to accomplish her goal. She became irritable with everyone, including herself, and she began to wonder what she was doing wrong.

One night Esther knelt in prayer and asked for guidance. Afterward, while lying awake, a startling thought [prompting of conscience] came to her. She realized that in focusing on her own perfection, she was focusing on herself and failing to love others, particularly her husband and children. She was being not loving, therefore not Christlike, but essentially selfish. She was trying to be sweet to her children, not freely, out of love for them, but because she saw it as a necessary part of *her* "perfection." Furthermore, she was trying to get a feeling of righteousness by forcing her husband and children to meet her ideal of perfection. When her children got in the way of her "perfect" routine, she blamed them for making her feel "imperfect," and she became irritated with them and treated them in a most unloving way. Likewise, if her husband did not meet her idea of perfection when he came home from work, she judged him as failing and was critical of him as a way of reinforcing her sense of her own righteousness.

Esther remembered the Savior's commandment to be perfect *as he is perfect* (see 3 Nephi 12:48). She realized that this perfection includes loving as he loved (see John 13:34), and she realized she had been pursuing the wrong goal.[4]

As with Esther, most of us who experience distortions of conscience, are overly anxious about issues of right and wrong. Part of this confusion could be that we haven't come to understand what it means to selflessly serve God and others, but have come to be more concerned with serving ourselves by showing the world how wonderfully competent we are. We are constantly on the run, doing a lot of things for a lot of people, and sometimes becoming physically ill in the process. Like Martha of New Testament times, those of us who struggle with these kinds of problems are "careful and troubled about many things" and "hath [not] chosen that good part" (Luke 10:41–42). Elder Neal A. Maxwell, of the Quorum of Twelve, has written: "A few in the Church are needlessly laden with programmed hyperactivity. They unwisely and unnecessarily exceed their strength and means, running faster than they are able (see D&C 10:4; Mosiah 4:27). Their fatiguing, Martha-like anxiety should yield more often to a Mary-like sense of proportion about what matters most; then the good part will not be taken from them (see Luke 10:41–42)."[5] A perfectionist's flurry of activity is often a type of "virtuous" excuse for avoiding other things we know to be right.

What matters most is doing what we know to be right, even if it means doing less or doing more than what is expected of us by our peers. I have come to believe that most of what I experience as anxiety and despair comes when I am doing too much or too little. I am either inappropriately trying to be someone I am not or I am not living up to who I am and what God would have me do. The tricky part of these satanic scenarios is that many of us who are doing too much believe we are not doing enough and those of us who aren't doing as much as we should are complaining that too much is being expected. These scenarios are often acted out in concert with a partner. Consider the following example from my life: Several years ago my wife, Kaye, asked me to rock our baby, Rachel, to sleep. She expressed her concern that she had so much to do and just couldn't seem to get it all done. I knew I should help, but I really wanted to watch a few minutes of the football game. I too had had an especially busy day and wanted to relax for just a few minutes. I quickly settled on a compromise; I could take Rachel to my room, watch the football game on the portable television, and rock her to sleep at the same time. A real win-win situation! I would miss the color screen, but what a small price to pay for being a good father and husband.

The problem came after a few minutes of watching the game. Rachel began to fuss. The thought came to my mind that if I turned the television off, walked with her and sang to her, she might be soothed. I knew it was the right thing to do, but did I do it? No, I spent the next thirty minutes struggling to watch the game and rock my daughter, all the while resenting the fact that I couldn't do what I wanted to!

After listening to Rachel continue to fuss, Kaye came into the room to see how I was doing. She suggested I try walking with Rachel and perhaps sing her a lullaby. I'm sorry to confess—I silently suffered Kaye's suggestions ("the guilty taketh the truth to be hard," 1 Nephi 16:2). I was self-righteously convinced that she didn't appreciate anything I was doing to help. After sensing my resistance, Kaye took Rachel from me, walked and sang to her and soon had her asleep.

Logically, I could argue that I had had a busy day and deserved to take a little break. I could even resent the fact that my wife wasn't being "sensitive to my needs" and was making "unrealistic demands" of me, after all, taking care of the baby was *her* primary responsibility, not mine. I had a grip on my weighty responsibilities, why couldn't she?

I had a lot of excuses (logical, emotional, and physical), but when it came down to the truth, I wasn't being true to what I knew to be right. The Savior described this kind of selfishness when he said: "For this people's heart is waxed gross, and their ears are dull of hearing, and their eyes they have closed; lest at any time they should see with their eyes, and hear with their ears, and should understand with their heart, and should be converted, and I should heal them" (Matthew 13:15; see also Jeremiah 5:21; Ezekiel 12:2). If we would only have the faith to act upon what we know to be right, we could begin to experience the healing spoken of in this verse. I've often wondered how much time, money, and happiness are wasted by our refusals to follow our promptings of conscience. It seems to take some of us longer than others to recognize that even simple promptings of conscience are expressions of God's will in accomplishing his selfless purposes. The commandments God has given us are expressions of who he is as well as what he would have us do. The Lord has taught us that all of what he does is centered on making it possible for us to have joy in this life and immortality and eternal life in the next (see Moses 1:39; 2 Nephi 2:25).

I believe that if we could see "things as they really are" (Jacob 4:13) we would realize that selfishness is the "root cause" for most of the problems we face in life. We put our own needs, wants, and desires above, before, and in place of the needs of others and the will of God. President Gordon B. Hinckley has stated: "There is no simple answer. I acknowledge that. But it appears to me that there are some obvious reasons that account for a very high percentage of these problems. I say this out of experience in dealing with such tragedies. I find selfishness to be the root cause of most of it."[6]

An interesting and inviting paradox is that it is only in losing ourselves in the service of God and others that we really find who we are and experience the personal peace and meaning we are seeking. The Savior taught: "For whosoever will save his life shall lose it: and whosoever will lose his life for my sake shall find it. For what is a man profited, if he shall gain the whole world, and lose his own soul? or what shall a man give in exchange for his soul?" (Matthew 16:25–26.)

It is through the light of Christ (conscience) that the Lord continually attempts to be one with us. He will never invite us to fall short (like I did with Rachel) or go (with Esther) "beyond the mark" (Jacob 4:14). We have been promised that if we are true to the light given us, greater light will follow: "That which is of God is light; and he that receiveth light, and continueth in God, receiveth more light; and that light groweth brighter and brighter until the perfect day" (D&C 50:24). This increase in light and knowledge is possible even for those who some consider "beyond hope." The Prophet Joseph Smith taught that "All the minds and spirits that God ever sent into the world are susceptible of enlargement."[7] This statement has had special meaning to me as I have worked with the mentally handicapped and the emotionally crippled.

Promptings of Conscience Usually Not Dramatic

Promptings of conscience are not usually dramatic experiences when we first sense them, but they can lead to miraculous transformations. One of the great lessons from the Old Testament is the story of the Syrian military leader Naaman and the Prophet Elisha. Naaman was leprous and sought Elisha to heal him of his malady. In response to Naaman's request, Elisha directed Naaman to wash himself in the river Jordan seven times. Naaman was insulted by the simplicity of Naaman's directive: "But Naaman was wroth, and went away, and said, Behold, I thought, He [Elijah] will surely come out to me, and stand, and call on the name of the Lord his God, and strike his hand over the place, and recover the leper. Are not Abana and Pharpar, rivers of Damascus, better than all the waters of Israel? may I not wash in them, and be clean? So he turned and went away in a rage." (2 Kings 5:11–12.)

Namman's followers recognized the fearful arrogance of their leader and suggested he reconsider the possibility that the cure which he was seeking didn't have to be dramatic or complex to be effective. "And his servants came near, and spake unto him, and said, My father, if the prophet had bid thee do some *great thing,* wouldest thou not have done it? how much rather then, when he saith to thee, Wash, and be clean? Then went he down, and dipped himself seven times in Jordan, according to the saying of the man of God: and his flesh came again like unto the flesh of a little child, and he was clean." (2 Kings 5:13–14; emphasis added.)

Sometimes, simple solutions like consistently spending more time with our spouse or children, praying regularly, having family home evening, fasting, and scripture reading are overlooked in favor of more dramatic cures involving doctors, hospitals, medications, and treatment programs. While these more dramatic and complicated solutions are sometimes necessary, we always need to remember the Lord's counsel that "out of small things proceedeth that which is great" (D&C 64:33).

Just as the scriptures contain accounts of lives being changed for the better in days of old, lives continue to be changed in the present as we come to understand and follow the directions the Lord gives us. Elder Spencer J. Condie, of the Seventy, has shared the following story of a man whose life was changed as he was true to his sense of right and wrong:

I know [a] good man who was reared in a family without the blessings of the gospel. Through a series of unfortunate events in his early youth, he was introduced to homosexuality, and gradually he became a prisoner of this addictive behavior.

One day two young missionaries knocked on his door and asked if he would be interested in learning of the restored gospel of Jesus Christ. In his heart of hearts he wanted to be freed from his prison of uncleanness, but feeling unable to change the direction his life had taken, he terminated the missionary discussions. Before leaving his apartment, the two elders left a copy of the Book of Mormon with him, and testified of its truthfulness.

My friend placed the book on his bookshelf and forgot about it for several years. He continued acting out his homosexual tendencies, assuming that such relationships would bring him happiness. But alas, with each passing year, his misery increased.

One day in the depths of despair, he scanned his bookshelf for something to read which might edify and uplift him and restore his self-worth. His eye caught hold of the book with a dark-blue cover, which the missionaries had given him several years before. He began to read. On the second page of this book, he read of Father Lehi's vision in which he was given a book to read, and "as he read, he was filled with the Spirit of the Lord" (1 Nephi 1:12). And as my good friend continued reading, he too was filled with the Spirit of the Lord.

He read King Benjamin's benedictory challenge to undergo a mighty change of heart—not a little change, but a mighty change. He was given hope by the comforting conversion stories of Enos, Alma, Ammon, and Aaron. He was also inspired by the account of the Savior's visit to the ancient Nephites. By the time he reached the final page of the Book of Mormon, he was prepared to accept Moroni's loving invitation to "come unto Christ, and be perfected in him, and deny yourselves of all ungodliness" (Moroni 10:32).

My friend contacted the Church and was taught the gospel and was baptized. Within a relatively short time, he married a lovely young woman, and they are the parents of several beautiful children. He and his wife are very dynamic and committed servants of the Lord, influencing many others for good.[8]

The solutions to the serious problems described in this story may sound simplistic to some, but it is important to remember that the days of miracles have not ceased (see Moroni 7:35).

Several years ago I worked with an individual who was trying to overcome his problems related to homosexual behavior. One day we were having a conversation about the origins of his problems and he said to me, "I'm sure I don't fully understand the arguments of those who say I was born this way, but what I do know is that I have been *born again* and no longer have the compulsive feelings and desires I once had." This individual hasn't simply learned to control his aberrant desires, but through the help of God has come to be free of them (see John 8:32). He has experienced what it means to be in "remission of sins" (Moroni 8:25).

There are some who would criticize these ideas and say that the gospel is fine for minor mishaps, but serious problems require serious solutions that are beyond "the simpleness of the way" (1 Nephi 17:41) taught in scripture. I respectfully disagree. It has been my experience that it isn't the gospel which is too simplistic, it is usually our understanding and faith in Christ that is insufficient. The sophistication of some won't allow them to believe and act upon simple solutions. Many have come to look at the alleged complexity of a problem as a reason for its existence as well as its resistance to change. Elder Neal A. Maxwell has observed:

It is true today; the simpleness, the easiness of the gospel is such that it causes people to perish because they can't receive it. We like variety. We like intellectual embroidery. We like complexity. We like complexity at times because it gives us an excuse for failure; that is, as you increase the complexity of a belief system, you provide more and more refuges for those who don't want to comply. You thereby increase the number of excuses that people can make for failure to comply, and you create a sophisticated intellectual structure which causes people to talk about the gospel instead of doing it. But the gospel of Jesus Christ really is not complex. It strips us of any basic excuse for noncompliance, and yet many of us are forever trying to make it more complex.[9]

Using "complexity" as a justification for sin is a part of what Jacob was teaching us when he warned of the dangers of going "beyond the mark": "But behold, the Jews were a stiffnecked people; and they despised the words of plainness, and killed the prophets, and sought for things that they could not understand. Wherefore, because of their blindness, which blindness came by looking beyond the mark, they must needs fall; for God hath taken away his plainness from them, and delivered unto them many things which they cannot understand, because they desired it. And because they desired it God hath done it, that they may stumble." (Jacob 4:14.)

It is my conviction that some of the confusion we experience concerning controversial issues such as homosexual behavior and gender equality comes because we have looked "beyond the mark" and have become blinded to the simpleness of the way outlined by God through his prophets. This isn't to say we shouldn't continue to do research in these areas and seek to understand all we can about them, but never should we do so at the expense of what the Lord has already revealed. The Prophet Joseph Smith once said: "And again we never inquire at the hand of God for special revelation only in case of there being no previous revelation to suit the case."[10]

While the problems most of us face aren't as serious as the same-sex attraction problem addressed earlier, each of us has problems we face from day to day which trouble us. Consider the following story of my wife and me as we sought to work through a problem with one of our children.[11] Several years ago we were dealing with one of the day-to-day problems experienced by most parents. Our son Jacob was becoming more and more aggressive with his younger sister, Jessica. We reasoned in part that Jake's problem could be due to his fascination with the "Masters of the Universe" cartoon characters. Such figures as He-Man, Sheera, and Skeletor had come to replace our family as the central figures in Jake's life. When Jake first began to play with these figurines we were amused as he, playing the role of He-Man, would rescue Jessi's Barbie dolls from the various villians who had abducted them. But soon our delight turned to distress as Jake became more and more aggressive in his talk and play. He soon changed from acting the part of the hero, He-Man, to playing the evil character, Skeletor. Jessi was upset not only because of the rough treatment she was receiving from Jake, but because Barbie was spending more and more time as a hostage because the good guys were no longer winning the battles. It seemed Jake and Jessi were constantly fighting. Kaye and I became increasingly concerned as to what we should do.

As a graduate student studying family science, I had been taught the various answers to dealing with these kinds of problems. But the problem I had was that many of the various solutions I had learned contradicted one another. Family-life educators, therapists, and writers coming from the Freudian tradition reasoned that Jake's aggressive behavior was to be expected and we ought to allow him to work out his "inner conflicts" through his play. Those coming from the behavioral perspective encouraged us to identify the behaviors we wanted to "extinguish" (eliminate) and those we wanted to "reinforce." We were then instructed to set up a schedule of rewards and punishments that would help us "manage" Jake and obtain the results we were looking for. Other writers explained that Jake's aggression was only a "stage" through which he was passing and not to worry. Still other "experts" encouraged us to reason with Jake and help him come to an understanding that his style of play was harmful both to himself and others.

Other writers, coming from an Adlerian perspective, which had become very popular in LDS circles, encouraged us to identify the goal behind Jake's misbehavior (like seeking attention). We were to then set up a series of "logical and natural consequences" that would help us deal with the "inferiority complex" we all supposedly have. Family systems theorists encouraged us to admit that Jake was simply the "identified patient" and that his misbehavior was a symptom of a problem with the way our family system was functioning. Was our family too rigid and in need of greater freedom and more opportunity of expression?

Our "politically correct" friends wouldn't allow their children to play with toys that encouraged violence and were somewhat disappointed we hadn't done the same. Should we forbid Jake from playing with such toys?

We responded by muddling along, dealing with each crisis as it came, but remaining tacitly concerned about Jake's increasing aggressiveness and resistance and our seeming inability to do much about it.

One day as I was listening to Jake and his friends do battle, I had the thought come into my mind that I should simply abandon my "conscientious objector" status and jump in and play! What if this really was a battle in which I had been called to participate? How would I, and how should I respond to the challenges of war? At first I tried to justify not playing. I thought of all the other more important things I had to do at the time and of how I really didn't want to give my support to such an abominable marketing charade as the "Masters of the Universe." But, for the first time in this particular sequence of events, my rationalizations weren't convincing, and I asked Jake if I could play. I don't know if he was more surprised or reluctant as his expression was a combination of both. He was probably surprised that I wanted to play and reluctant to allow me to play because I would probably get in the way of the fun he and his friends were having. Whatever his thoughts were, Jake responded by saying, "okay, Dad, you can be Man-at-Arms." Man-at-Arms was one of the good guys, who wasn't one of the main players (kind of symbolic of my role as Jake's parent at the time). After a few light skirmishes, I soon found myself without much to do. If you weren't in the process of capturing or being captured the game was somewhat meaningless. This changed quickly, however, as Skeletor abducted Barbie. I knew it was my duty to rescue her, which after a heroic battle, I did. I also arrested Skeletor and took him to my newly constructed military prison (Grandma's antique end table). Much to Jake's chagrin, I then began reading to Skeletor from a Book of Mormon that was nearby. Jake voiced his protest, "Dad, you can't do that . . . these guys aren't churchy!" Between thwarting various rescue attempts by Jake and the other disciples of doom, I continued to explain the gospel to Skeletor. After some time had passed, I informed Jake and his friends that Skeletor had agreed to be baptized. Jake continued his protest, but his resistance soon softened as he watched me fill a large Tupperware bowl with water and invite the other "Masters of the Universe" characters to attend Skeletor's baptismal service. We then "baptized" Skeletor.

I realize to some, holding a mock baptism may sound like sacrilege, but my change of heart, which allowed me to enter Jake's world and the subsequent baptism of Skeletor, marked a change in my relationship with my son. I gave my heart to Jake and he gave his to me. No longer did I see Jake as my enemy, but as my son and brother whom I have the privilege of introducing to *The* Master of the universe—Jesus Christ. Today, if you were to ask Jake to describe his dad, he would probably tell you this story with a mixture of incredulousness and delight.

As we come to learn the language of conscience, we must also take heed that we ". . . do not judge that which is evil to be of God, or that which is good and of God to be of the devil" (Moroni 7:14). Parents often indulge their children in the name of mercy. In reality, indulgence, or "unconditional love" as it is sometimes called, is a cheap counterfeit of mercy requiring very little of the parent's time and/or energy. On the other hand, mercy requires that an unfeigned price be paid. A parent can't simply spend "quality time" with their children and be fulfilling their responsibilities. President Howard W. Hunter taught us that "effective family leadership . . . requires both quantity and quality time."[12] Conversely, parents could spend too much time with their children as a diversion from other things they know they need to be doing. Something doesn't have to be inherently evil to be wrong.

Another example of sin and selfishness masquerading as revelation is often found in relation to the decisions concerning marriage and divorce. I am familiar with a couple of different situations where individuals have supposedly received revelation (while attending the temple) that they were to divorce their spouse and marry another. While I do not doubt that the Lord could direct someone to divorce, I believe that such a revelation would come in a very unique circumstance and not simply because of selfish reasons such as "irreconcilable differences" or because one has "fallen out of love."[13]

Another way of identifying our conscience is to ask and follow through on the question, "What would the Lord have me do?" It is a simple suggestion with profound implications. President Howard W. Hunter counseled: "Let us follow the Son of God in all ways and in all walks of life. Let us make him our exemplar and our guide. We should at every opportunity ask ourselves, 'What would Jesus do?' and then be more courageous to act upon the answer. . . . To the extent that our mortal powers permit, we should make every effort to become like Christ—the one perfect and sinless example this world has ever seen."[14]

Striving to do the "right thing" or trying to do what the Savior would do doesn't always mean doing more. Sometimes the right thing is to do nothing. I have always been interested in Mark's description of the Savior seeking solitude and rest on the coast of the Mediterranean Sea: "And from thence he [Jesus] arose, and went into the borders of Tyre and Sidon, and entered into a house, and would that no man should come unto him. But he could not deny them; for he had compassion upon all men." (JST, Mark 7:22–23.) Note the differences between the text above from the Joseph Smith Translation and the same text below from the King James Translation: "And from thence he arose, and went into the borders of Tyre and Sidon, and entered into an house, and would have no man know it: but he could not be hid" (KJV, Mark 7:24). The King James translation seems to indicate that the Savior was attempting to be alone, but could not successfully evade his followers. The Joseph Smith Translation teaches us that the Savior did indeed seek time alone, but because of his perfect love for others he was always open to their needs.

We learn a similar lesson about the rightness of rest and diversion from William Allred's description of an incident in the life of Joseph Smith: "He [Joseph Smith] was preaching once, and he said it tried some of the pious folks to see him play ball with the boys. He then related a story of a certain prophet who was sitting under the shade of a tree amusing himself in some way, when a hunter came along with his bow and arrow, and reproved him. The prophet asked him if he kept his bow strung up all the time. The hunter answered that he did not. The prophet asked why, and he said it would lose its elasticity if he did. The prophet said it was just so with his mind, he did not want it strung up all the time."[15] Personally, inspiration seems to flow most freely when I am seeking to serve others and not myself. Some of my most valuable, revelatory experiences have been while I have been teaching my students or ward members, playing with my children, washing the supper dishes, or serving in the temple.

Many of us consider revelation to be something only prophets experience, but the scriptures invite us to understand that each of us can receive revelation for our individual lives. Moses taught: "would God that all the Lord's people were prophets, and that the Lord would put his spirit upon them!" (Numbers 11:29.)

It is my conviction that our Heavenly Father is attempting to communicate with us day by day and moment by moment through our conscience, if we will but listen. President Spencer W. Kimball wrote: "If any of us wish to have more precise prescriptions for ourselves in terms of what we can do to have more abundant lives, all we usually need to do is to consult our conscience."[16]

NOTES

1. Boyd K. Packer, "The Law and the Light," *The Book of Mormon: Jacob Through Words of Mormon, to Learn with Joy*, eds. Monte Nyman and Charles Tate, Jr. (Provo: Religious Studies Center, Brigham Young University, 1990), pp. 3–4.

2. I am grateful to my colleague Professor C. Terry Warner for helping me to come to a better understanding of both conscience and sin.

3. "Lecture Fourth," *Lectures on Faith* (Salt Lake City: Deseret Book Co., 1985), pp. 51–52.

4. In *Teach Them Correct Principles: A Study in Family Relations* (Salt Lake City: The Church of Jesus Christ of Latter-day Saints, 1987), p. 7.

5. Neal A. Maxwell, *Men and Women of Christ*, (Salt Lake City: Bookcraft, 1991), p. 3.

6. Gordon B. Hinckley, "What God Hath Joined Together," *Ensign*, May 1991, p. 73.

7. Joseph Smith, *Teachings of the Prophet Joseph Smith*, comp. Joseph Fielding Smith (Salt Lake City: Deseret Book Co., 1976), p. 354.

8. Spencer J. Condie, "A Mighty Change of Heart," *Ensign*, November 1993, pp. 16–17.

9. Neal A. Maxwell, *"For the Power Is In Them . . ." Mormon Musings* (Salt Lake City: Deseret Book Co., 1970), pp. 48–49.

10. Joseph Smith, *Teachings of the Prophet Joseph Smith*, p. 22.

11. A similar version of this story appears in Daniel K Judd, "The Lord's Plan for Parents and Children," in Douglas E. Brinley and Daniel K Judd, eds., *Eternal Families* (Salt Lake City: Bookcraft, 1996), pp. 66–89.

12. Howard W. Hunter, "Being a Righteous Husband and Father," *Ensign*, November 1994, p. 50.

13. See James E. Faust, "Father, Come Home," *Ensign*, May 1993, pp. 35–37 for a discussion of "just causes" for divorce.

14. Howard W. Hunter, " 'What Manner of Men Ought Ye to Be?' " *Ensign*, May 1994, p. 64.

15. "Recollections of the Prophet Joseph Smith," *Juvenile Instructor*, 27 (1892), p. 471.

16. Spencer W. Kimball, *The Teachings of Spencer W. Kimball*, ed. Edward L. Kimball (Salt Lake City: Bookcraft, 1982), p. 155.

3

O that cunning plan of the evil one! O the vainness, and the frailties, and the foolishness of men! When they are learned they think they are wise, and they hearken not unto the counsel of God, for they set it aside, supposing they know of themselves, wherefore, their wisdom is foolishness and it profiteth them not. And they shall perish. But to be learned is good if they hearken unto the counsels of God.
—2 Nephi 9:28–29

REASON AND REVELATION

One of the major contributing factors to apostasy in the early Christian church was the influence of various aspects of Greek philosophy. In addition to arguing that God is without body, parts, or passions, and that many, if not most, of the historical events described in the Bible were simply myths, some Greek philosophers taught that reason should take the place of revelation as the directing influence in people's lives.[1] This influence has continued to the present and has come to permeate our culture. Many people have come to base their most important decisions on "what the research says" or on the opinions of others, and have excluded the influence of revelation from their lives. While information gleaned from scientific research can be a blessing, it is critical that we continue to understand the importance of revelation. This becomes especially important when there are conflicting opinions as to what we ought to do in a given situation. Sometimes the shrill voices of reason can drown out the still small voice of revelation (see 1 Kings 19:12). Furthermore, following our own sense of right and wrong and attempting to follow the Lord's counsel might not always be consistent with research evidence or with what others might consider to be the reasonable choice. An example of this conflict is demonstrated in the present debate over alcohol consumption and heart disease. The Lord has instructed us that we are to refrain from drinking alcoholic beverages (see D&C 89:7), but groups such as the National Institute on Alcohol Abuse and Alcoholism have stated that moderate drinking can be beneficial to one's health.[2] Even if it is accurate to say that a few ounces of alcohol a day will prevent heart disease, we know it was mankind's spiritual health and not his physical condition that the Lord was describing when he stated that in the last days "men's hearts shall fail them. . . . And the love of men shall wax cold, and iniquity shall abound." (D&C 45:26–27.)

While there is ample evidence concerning the dangers of alcohol consumption, perhaps the most serious consequences are spiritual and emotional, not physical. It is imperative we understand that what is right might not always be consistent with what the experts have to say. President Joseph Fielding Smith wrote of the danger of relying solely on the power of intellect:

> The worship of reason, of false philosophy, is greater now than it was [in the past]. Men are depending upon their own research to find out God, and that which they cannot discover and which they cannot demonstrate to their satisfaction through their own research and their natural senses, they reject. They are not seeking for the Spirit of the Lord; they are not striving to know God in the manner in which he has marked out by which he may be known; but they are walking in their own way, believing in their own man-made philosophies, teaching the doctrines of devils and not the doctrines of the Son of God.[3]

This isn't to say that reason and intellect should be rejected as sources of truth, only that reason shouldn't be exercised without regard to the wisdom of God. The Lord told Nephi that we should not "hearken unto the precepts of men, save their precepts shall be given by the power of the Holy Ghost" (2 Nephi 28:31). Nephi's brother Jacob taught that "to be learned is good if they hearken unto the counsels of God" (2 Nephi 9:29). Elder Hugh B. Brown counseled us that research and revelation can provide truth:

The Church of Jesus Christ of Latter-day Saints accepts newly revealed truth, whether it comes through direct revelation or from study and research. We deny the common conception of reality that distinguishes radically between the natural and the supernatural, between the temporal and the eternal, between the sacred and the secular. For us, there is no order of reality that is utterly different in character from the world of which we are a part, that is separated from us by an impassable gulf. We do not separate our daily mundane tasks and interests from the meaning and substance of religion. We recognize the spiritual in all phases and aspects of living and realize that this life is an important part of eternal life.[4]

Truth can be found in a laboratory or in Leviticus, in a textbook as well as on a mountain top, but not all truth is of equal importance. The critical point is that we need to make "righteous judgment" (JST, Matthew 7:1–2) of the knowledge we obtain, whatever its origin. Joseph Smith taught that "If there is anything virtuous, lovely, or of good report or praiseworthy, we seek after these things" (Articles of Faith 1:13).

The prophet Mormon taught that the way to make correct judgments between what is right and wrong "is as plain, that ye may know with a perfect knowledge, as the daylight is from the dark night. . . . For every thing which inviteth to do good, and to persuade to believe in Christ, is sent forth by the power and gift of Christ; wherefore ye may know with a perfect knowledge it is of God." (Moroni 7:15–16.)

This isn't to say, however, that we will always be able to discern right from wrong immediately. From the Doctrine and Covenants we read: "But as you cannot always judge the righteous, or as you cannot always tell the wicked from the righteous, therefore I say unto you, *hold your peace* until I shall see fit to make all things known unto the world concerning the matter" (D&C 10:37; emphasis added). There will be times when we will need to exercise patience and faith as we "wait upon the Lord" (2 Nephi 18:17) for the understanding we are seeking. But in our waiting, it is important that we are not guilty of the same mistake as Oliver Cowdery when he didn't do his part in preparation for receiving answers to his questions concerning the translation of the Book of Mormon. The Lord counseled Brother Cowdery: "Behold, you have not understood; you have supposed that I would give it unto you, when you took no thought save it was to ask me. But, behold, I say unto you, that you must study it out in your mind; then you must ask me if it be right, and if it is right I will cause that your bosom shall burn within you; therefore, you shall feel that it is right." (D&C 9:7–9.) Oftentimes, revelation is more of a process than a singular event.

There are those who have sought to fragment reason from revelation. Much of the intellectual tradition that exists in the world today comes from those who have rejected revelation and have come to revere reason as the sole source of truth. But just as faithless intellectualism is a threat to the pursuit of truth, mindless mysticism is also a dangerous counterfeit. Both are tools of the adversary, designed to confuse and eventually destroy. The Lord has instructed us that both reason and revelation are conduits through which he communicates. "Yea, behold, I will tell you in your mind and in your heart, by the Holy Ghost, which shall come upon you and which shall dwell in your heart" (D&C 8:2). In addition to seeking to understand and fulfill the Lord's instructions, we are also invited to think and feel for ourselves in using our own experience and agency to build the kingdom. "For behold, it is not meet that I should command in all things; for he that is compelled in all things, the same is a slothful and not a wise servant; wherefore he receiveth no reward. Verily I say, men should be anxiously engaged in a good cause, and do many things of their own free will, and bring to pass much righteousness; for the power is in them, wherein they are agents unto themselves. And inasmuch as men do good they shall in nowise lose their reward." (D&C 58:26–28.)

A powerful example of the Lord teaching one of his children the process of revelation is found in the Book of Mormon account of the Lord's schooling of the brother of Jared. The Lord gave the brother of Jared detailed directions concerning the building of barges which would take him and his family from the old world to the new (see Ether 2:16–18). The Lord also gave him specific instructions concerning the ventilation of the barges (see Ether 2:19–20). But when the brother of Jared inquired of the Lord as to what he should do to solve the problem of there being no light in the barges, the Lord answered him:

> *What will ye that I should do* that ye may have light in your vessels? For behold, ye cannot have windows, for they will be dashed in pieces; neither shall ye take fire with you, for ye shall not go by the light of fire.
>
> For behold, ye shall be as a whale in the midst of the sea; for the mountain waves shall dash upon you. Nevertheless, I will bring you up again out of the depths of the sea; for the winds have gone forth out of my mouth, and also the rains and the floods have I sent forth.
>
> And behold, I prepare you against these things; for ye cannot cross this great deep save I prepare you against the waves of the sea, and the winds which have gone forth, and the floods which shall come. Therefore *what will ye that I should prepare* for you that ye may have light when ye are swallowed up in the depths of the sea? (Ether 2:23–25; emphasis added.)

The Lord responds by listing several alternatives that wouldn't be useful and then asks the brother of Jared, "What will ye that I should prepare for you?" The brother of Jared, using his own experience and ability, arrives at a solution and presents sixteen stones to the Lord for his blessing. The Lord then literally empowers the brother of Jared's solution by touching his finger to the stones (see Ether 3:1–6).

It has been my experience that the Lord often deals with each of us in this very same way. He responds to many of our challenges with specific instructions on how to handle them. Many of the answers are available to us even before we ask the questions. The Lord answers other questions by asking us, "What will ye that I should do?"

As a husband, parent, and bishop, I have learned that sometimes the Lord will make very clear, to both myself and those I am working with, what we should do in answer to a particular problem we are facing. Other times, he will leave the decision to us and then "touch his finger" to our decision. I believe that it is even possible to make a relatively poor choice and have the Lord make it right if we are being humble, worthy, and faithful in our attempts to fulfill our responsibilities.

Many of the questions we have concerning the various challenges we face in life should very well include answers we come to on our own or through the suggestions of others, but never should we seek to employ them independent of the Lord's blessing. We can always have confidence in the knowledge that our Heavenly Father loves us and wants to help us deal with the challenges we face. As the Savior counseled his ancient apostles:

> And I say unto you, Ask, and it shall be given you; seek, and ye shall find; knock, and it shall be opened unto you.
>
> For every one that asketh receiveth; and he that seeketh findeth; and to him that knocketh it shall be opened.
>
> If a son shall ask bread of any of you that is a father, will he give him a stone? or if he ask a fish, will he for a fish give him a serpent?
>
> Or if he shall ask an egg, will he offer him a scorpion?
>
> If ye then, being evil, know how to give good gifts unto your children: how much more shall your heavenly Father give the Holy Spirit to them that ask him? (Luke 11:9–13.)

Joy in Their Works for a Season

While there is some truth in most, if not all, the various theories of the human behavior, most do not focus on what the revelations tell us are most important—a change of heart. Neither do these theories focus on the proper means of this transformation—"[yielding] to the enticings of the Holy Spirit and [putting] off the natural man . . . through the atonement of Christ the Lord" (Mosiah 3:19).

I was once told by a friend that he no longer needed the Church. This man, who was a high priest and had been a member of the Church most of his life, told me that he had found a support group that filled his needs much better than the Church ever had or ever could. He reasoned that he liked his support group because it made no demands on his time and the people were accepting of anything he said or did and that he had calculated that the group therapy fee was less expensive than paying tithing! While wanting to be respectful of this fellow and the difficulties he had experienced, as his bishop I also felt it was my responsibility to warn him that the joy he had found was deceptive and temporary. We read the following verse together from the Book of Mormon: "But if it be not built upon my gospel, and is built upon the works of men, or upon the works of the devil, verily I say unto you they have joy in their works for a season, and by and by the end cometh, and they are hewn down and cast into the fire, from whence there is no return" (3 Nephi 27:11).

Any philosophy, therapy, or way of life, no matter how reasonable, that is not grounded in or consistent with the truths of the gospel of Jesus Christ is destined to eventual failure. It took about a year for the fellow I have been describing to realize that his therapy group wasn't the answer to his problems. While he continued for a time to be "tossed to and fro, and carried about with every wind of doctrine" (Ephesians 4:14) by going from one psychological theory to the next, he eventually came back into the Church and is making progress towards appreciating the elegance, truth, and power of the gospel of Jesus Christ.

Hopefully, each one of us will come to fully appreciate the power of revelation in addressing the various problems we face, for we know that "He will yet reveal many great and important things pertaining to the Kingdom of God" (Articles of Faith 1:9) and our own individual lives.

NOTES

1. See Neal A. Maxwell, "From the Beginning," *Ensign,* November 1993, pp. 18–20, for an introduction to the influence of Greek philosophy on the early Christian church.

2. Adam Feibelman, "Revised Alcohol Guidelines Become Official," *Alcoholism & Drug Abuse Weekly,* 1 January 1996, p. 4.

3. Joseph Fielding Smith, *Doctrines of Salvation,* comp. Bruce R. McConkie, 3 vols. (Salt Lake City: Bookcraft, 1954–56), 3:275.

4. Hugh B. Brown, in Conference Report, April 1964, pp. 81–82.

But ye are commanded in all things to ask of God, . . .
that ye may not be seduced by evil spirits, or doctrines
of devils, or the commandments of men; for some
are of men, and others of devils.
—D&C 46:7

THE DOCTRINES OF GOD, THE PHILOSOPHIES OF MEN, AND THE SUBTLETIES OF SATAN

Discerning between the teachings of God, the philosophies of men, and the subtleties of the devil is not always easy to do, but a latter-day prophet has given us wise counsel concerning the importance of using the Book of Mormon as a standard by which we can discern truth from error. President Ezra Taft Benson once stated:

> The Book of Mormon brings men to Christ through two basic means. First, it tells in a plain manner of Christ and His gospel. It testifies of His divinity and of the necessity for a Redeemer and the need of our putting trust in Him. It bears witness of the Fall and the Atonement and the first principles of the gospel, including our need of a broken heart and a contrite spirit and a spiritual rebirth. It proclaims we must endure to the end in righteousness and live the moral life of a Saint.
>
> Second, the Book of Mormon exposes the enemies of Christ. It confounds false doctrines and lays down contention (see 1 Nephi 3:12). It fortifies the humble followers of Christ against the evil designs, strategies, and doctrines of the devil in

our day. The type of apostates in the Book of Mormon are similar to the type we have today. God, with His infinite fore-knowledge, so molded the Book of Mormon that we might see the error and know how to combat false educational, po-litical, religious, and philosophical concepts of our time. ("The Book of Mormon Is the Word of God," Regional Rep-resentatives Seminar, Salt Lake City, Utah, 4 April 1986.)[1]

The Book of Mormon contains multiple prophetic warnings concerning the false philosophies that would exist in our day. Nephi recorded several of Satan's strategies in the following:

> For behold, at that day [our day] shall he [Satan] rage in the hearts of the children of men, and stir them up to anger against that which is good.
> And others will he pacify, and lull them away into carnal security, that they will say: All is well in Zion; yea, Zion pros-pereth, all is well—and thus the devil cheateth their souls, and leadeth them away carefully down to hell.
> And behold, others he flattereth away, and telleth them there is no hell; and he saith unto them: I am no devil, for there is none—and thus he whispereth in their ears, until he grasps them with his awful chains, from whence there is no de-liverance. . . .
> Therefore, wo be unto him that is at ease in Zion!
> Wo be unto him that crieth: All is well!
> Yea, wo be unto him that hearkeneth unto the precepts of men, and denieth the power of God, and the gift of the Holy Ghost! (2 Nephi 28:20–26.)

While there are those among us who "rage" against the teachings of Christ and his servants and others who have come to believe that the devil is a mythical being, our prophets have been even more concerned with Satan's tactic of lulling us away into carnal security. Brigham Young taught: "The worst fear that I have about this people is that they will get rich in this country, forget God and His people, wax fat, and kick them-selves out of the Church and go to hell. This people will stand mobbing, robbing, poverty, and all manner of persecution, and be true. But my greater fear for them is that they cannot stand wealth; and yet they have to be tried with riches, for they will become the richest people on this earth."[2] The *carnal security* (see 2 Nephi 28:21) spoken of by Nephi and Brigham Young is an interesting phrase. The word *carnal* pertains to "things of the flesh," or "of the world," and *security* means "to be safe."[3] In other words, *carnal security* implies that we are safe, pertaining to things of the world. Most of us desire to be safe, comfortable, and to have sufficient of the world's goods to satisfy our needs, but the problem comes when our sense of temporal security leads us to idolatry. President Spencer W. Kimball explained:

> As I study ancient scripture, I am more and more convinced that there is significance in the fact that the commandment "Thou shalt have no other gods before me" is the first of the Ten Commandments.
>
> Few men have ever knowingly and deliberately chosen to reject God and his blessings. Rather, we learn from the scriptures that because the exercise of faith has always appeared to be more difficult than relying on things more immediately at hand, carnal man has tended to transfer his trust in God to material things. . . .
>
> Many people spend most of their time working in the service of a self-image that includes sufficient money, stocks, bonds, investment portfolios, property, credit cards, furnishings, automobiles, and the like to *guarantee* carnal security throughout, it is hoped, a long and happy life. Forgotten is the fact that our assignment is to use these many resources in our families and quorums to build up the kingdom of God—to further the missionary effort and the genealogical and temple work; to raise our children up as fruitful servants unto the Lord; to bless others in every way, that they may also be fruitful. Instead, we expend these blessings on our own desires.[4]

In addition to demonstrating how carnal security represents an idolatrous worship of material posessions, the Book of Mormon contains an account of a man who sought the social security provided by the praise of others. "And I have taught his [the devil's] words; and I taught them because they were pleasing unto the carnal mind; and I taught them, even until I had much success, insomuch that I verily believed that they were true; and for this cause I withstood the truth, even until I have brought this great curse upon me" (Alma 30:53).

Korihor became entangled in Satan's ploy of pragmatism. While the scriptures teach us that "by their fruits ye shall know them" (Matthew 7:20), it isn't always possible to judge something to be right or wrong by its public acceptance or immediate consequences. This was the problem encountered by the people during the time of Malachi. The following is a dialogue between the Lord and the children of Israel concerning the wealth of the wicked and the suffering of the righteous: "Your words have been stout against me, saith the Lord. Yet ye say, What have we spoken so much against thee? Ye have said, It is vain to serve God: and what profit is it that we have kept his ordinance, and that we have walked mournfully before the Lord of hosts? And now we call the proud happy; yea, they that work wickedness are set up; yea, they that tempt God are even delivered." (Malachi 3:13–15.) The Lord then describes how the day will soon come that both the wicked and the righteous will receive their eternal reward: "Then they that feared the Lord spake often one to another: and the Lord hearkened, and heard it, and a book of remembrance was written before him for them that feared the Lord, and that thought upon his name. And they shall be mine, saith the Lord of hosts, in that day when I make up my jewels; and I will spare them, as a man spareth his own son that serveth him. Then shall ye return, and discern between the righteous and the wicked, between him that serveth God and him that serveth him not." (Malachi 3:16–18.)

It has always interested me that this dialogue follows the Lord's invitation to "prove me now herewith, saith the Lord of hosts, if I will not open you the windows of heaven, and pour you out a blessing, that there shall not be room enough to receive it" (Malachi 3:10). Promised blessings will come, surely as day follows night, but in the due time of the Lord.

Not long ago I was visiting with a friend who had been physically abused by her parents when she was a child. This woman is active in the Church, has been in therapy most of her adult life, but continues to experience emotional pain that is nearly crippling. During our conversation she asked me the question, "When will the pain go away?" I told her that while I knew that the healing of her afflictions was possible, it was improbable that either of us could know when. She then shared with me her confusion over a book she was reading. Apparently, what she had read in this book had led her to believe that if she was faithful and kept the commandments she could select a particular date and "bind the Lord" as to the time of her deliverance from suffering. I told her that in my opinion, she had misunderstood what the author was attempting to communicate, or what the author was teaching was false. While the Lord has taught us, "I, the Lord am bound when ye do what I say; when ye do not what I say, ye have no promise" (D&C 82:10), it is not for us to "counsel the Lord, but to take counsel from his hand" (Jacob 4:10) pertaining to the timing of the blessings which we are seeking.

As faithful and valiant as was the Apostle Paul, he prayed repeatedly to have his "thorn in the flesh" removed, but the Lord saw fit to answer Paul's prayer by allowing his affliction to continue:

> And lest I should be exalted above measure through the abundance of the revelations, there was given to me a thorn in the flesh, the messenger of Satan to buffet me, lest I should be exalted above measure.
>
> For this thing *I besought the Lord thrice, that it might depart from me.*
>
> And he said unto me, My grace is sufficient for thee: for my strength is made perfect in weakness. Most gladly therefore will I rather glory in my infirmities, that the power of Christ may rest upon me.

Therefore I take pleasure in infirmities, in reproaches, in necessities, in persecutions, in distresses for Christ's sake: for when I am weak, then am I strong. (2 Corinthians 12:7–10; emphasis added.)

Was it Paul's lack of faith that prevented him from having his affliction removed? Couldn't he have "bound the Lord" to heal him of his infirmities? We must remember that the powers of heaven are unleashed when our prayers are focused on the Lord's will and not our own. The Lord has clearly taught, "He that asketh in the Spirit asketh according to the will of God; wherefore it is done even as he asketh" (D&C 46:30). Elder Neal A. Maxwell has written:

Petitioning in prayer has taught me, again and again, that the vault of heaven with all its blessings is to be opened only by a combination lock. One tumbler falls when there is faith, a second when there is personal righteousness; the third and final tumbler falls only when what is sought is, in God's judgment— not ours—right for us. Sometimes we pound on the vault door for something we want very much and wonder why the door does not open. We would be very spoiled children if that vault door opened any more easily than it does. I can tell, looking back, that God truly loves me by inventorying the petitions He has refused to grant me. Our rejected petitions tell us much about ourselves but also much about our flawless Father.[5]

Deceiving the Very Elect

The scriptures warn us that in the last days there will exist many who would attempt to decieve us. "For there shall arise false Christs, and false prophets, and shall shew great signs and wonders; insomuch that, if it were possible, they shall deceive the very elect" (Matthew 24:24). The Prophet Joseph Smith added these significant words to Matthew's account, "who are the elect, according to the covenant" (JST, Matthew 24:24). In other words, the people whom the false Christs, and false prophets will be attempting to deceive are the covenant members of The Church of Jesus Christ of Latter-day Saints. President Harold B. Lee warned: "Unless every member of this Church gains for himself an unshakable testimony of the divinity of this Church, he will be among those who will be deceived in this day when the 'elect according to the covenant' are going to be tried and tested. Only those will survive who have gained for themselves that testimony."[6]

Who are these false Christs and false prophets among us, and what are the great signs and wonders they are using in attempting to deceive us? In addition to the obvious false Christs that appear in the media from time to time, I believe the false Christs and false prophets spoken of in this verse are much more sophisticated and dangerous than those who publically (or privately) announce they are literally the Christ. Elder Bruce R. McConkie has written: "A false Christ is not a person. It is a false system of worship, a false church, a false cult that says: 'Lo, here is salvation; here is the doctrine of Christ. Come and believe thus and so, and ye shall be saved.' It is any concept or philosophy that says that redemption, salvation, sanctification, justification, and all of the promised rewards can be gained in any way except that set forth by the apostles and prophets."[7] The terms *false Christs, false prophets, false preachers,* and *false teachers* represent the false philosophies promulgated by those who espouse them. President Lee counseled: "False prophets and christs, as foretold by the Savior, may come to deceive us not alone in the name of religion, but . . . they may come under the label of politicians or of social planners or so-called economists, deceitful in their offerings of a kind of salvation which may come under such guise."[8]

Trojan Horse Psychology

Another example of an area which can offer the deceitful kind of salvation spoken of by President Lee, is found in what some promote as counseling and psychotherapy. While I believe faithful and competent psychologists, psychiatrists, and social workers can play a legitimate role in addressing the problems we face, I also believe we need to exercise caution in doing so. Having been involved in the world of counseling for several years, I know that some forms of therapy are destructive and can lead one to doubt the existence of God, the inspired guidance of leaders, and other truths of the Restoration. If we allow our therapist to replace our priesthood leaders, the therapist's counsel to take the place of personal revelation, and the philosophy of psychology to replace the doctrines of the Restoration, we have been deceived. I am concerned that some of us see the practice of psychotherapy as a great blessing, while in reality this "gift," in some cases, may very well be a Trojan horse. Elder Richard G. Scott (speaking specifically on the treatment of sexual abuse) addressed some of the dangers to avoid if we receive professional counseling:

> I caution you not to participate in two improper therapeutic practices that may cause you more harm than good. They are: Excessive probing into every minute detail of your past experiences, particularly when this involves penetrating dialogue in group discussion; and blaming the abuser for every difficulty in your life.
>
> While some discovery is vital to the healing process, the almost morbid probing into details of past acts, long buried and mercifully forgotten, can be shattering. There is no need to pick at healing wounds to open them and cause them to fester. The Lord and his teachings can help you without destroying self-respect.
>
> There is another danger. Detailed leading questions that probe your past may unwittingly trigger thoughts that are more imagination or fantasy than reality. They could lead to condemnation of another for acts that were not committed. While likely few in number, I know of cases where such therapy has caused great injustice to the innocent from unwittingly stimulated accusations that were later proven false. Memory, particularly adult memory of childhood experiences, is fallible. Remember, false accusation is also a sin.[9]

The gospel of Jesus Christ is the Lord's plan for our happiness in this life and exaltation in the world to come. Any theory or philosophy that leads people away from Christ or his teachings has to be considered anti-Christ. The Apostle Paul warned: "Beware lest any man spoil you through philosophy and vain deceit, after the tradition of men, after the rudiments of the world, and not after Christ" (Colossians 2:8).

As a missionary I had the privilege of serving under Elder Hartman Rector Jr., of the First Quorum of Seventy. One of the many things President Rector taught me was that the gospel of Jesus Christ has a power to change people's lives that is superior to any other philosophy or therapy. He was fond of saying, "The gospel of Jesus Christ is to make bad men good, good men better, and better men better than ever before."[10] I observed President Rector help work miracles in the lives of missionaries and others who had not been helped through traditional counseling and psychotherapy.

Again, I am not saying that all of the philosophies of men are evil and we ought to shun them, only that we need to exercise caution when we encounter them. While there is much to be learned from the wisdom of the world, sometimes we can become so engrossed with it that we begin to judge the principles of the gospel by the philosophies of men rather than the other way around. Elder Boyd K. Packer gave the following counsel concerning the relationship of the philosophies of man and the doctrines of God:

> I have come to believe that it is the tendency for many members of the Church who spend a great deal of time in academic research to begin to judge the Church, its doctrine, organization, and leadership, present and past, by the principles of their own profession. Ofttimes this is done unwittingly, and some of it, perhaps, is not harmful.
>
> It is an easy thing for a man with extensive academic training to measure the Church using the principles he has been taught in his professional training as his standard. In my mind it ought to be the other way around. A member of the Church

ought always, particularly if he is pursuing extensive academic studies, to judge the professions of man against the revealed word of the Lord.[11]

While the majority of Church members do not spend their time in academic research, many devote a significant amount of time to reading self-help books pertaining to personal and relationship issues. While these books may contain some truths, they always need to be compared against the standard of truth, the gospel of Jesus Christ. If what we read isn't consistent with what the Lord and his prophets have taught and what we know to be true through the Holy Ghost, we should follow the Apostle Paul's counsel: "from such turn away" (2 Timothy 3:5). Being true to what we know to be right will provide us with increased faith in the Lord and confidence in our ability to identify and follow his directing influence.

In the following, the prophet Mormon summarized for us the great sorrow or rejoicing experienced by all who either follow or reject the light of Christ: "And thus we see the great reason of sorrow, and also of rejoicing—sorrow because of death and destruction among men, and joy because of the *light of Christ* unto life" (Alma 28:14; emphasis added).

When I was a teenager, my aged grandfather, Frank Levi Farnsworth, moved into our home with my family and me. He prided himself in being an atheist and from the beginning began to challenge my religious beliefs. On a regular basis, Grandpa Frank would make disparaging comments about the Church, the Book of Mormon, and some of the Church leaders he had known over the years; I would usually respond by passionately defending what I felt was right. During the years we spent living in the same house we debated everything from the atonement of Christ to the establishment of Zion.

Motivated by a discussion we once had about the Word of Wisdom, I once even went so far as to replace his brand of coffee with a decaffeinated brand without him knowing. I took prideful pleasure in observing him drink his cup of coffee each morning and noting that it took several weeks before he made any mention of his coffee tasting different. I am ashamed to admit it, but in time, I dismissed my grandfather as an apostate and didn't have much to do with him. Little did I realize that one day I would come to understand the profound blessing he had been in my life.

When I was serving as a missionary I had the opportunity of laboring on the campus of San Diego State University. During my time there my companion and I were constantly getting in conversations with both professors and students about the Church and our beliefs. From these discussions we were able to meet, teach, and baptize several people.

Late one night, after an especially successful baptismal service, I was sitting in my apartment feeling good about the work I had been doing when I began to have thoughts of Grandpa Farnsworth fill my mind. As I contemplated the discussions we had had, these words came to my mind, "Dan, judge me not, for I have taught you well." It was with humility that I realized that the opposition my grandfather had provided was a major part of why I had been so successful while serving on campus. I had never been asked a question by a student or a professor that my grandfather and I hadn't thoroughly discussed on a prior occasion. Without my realizing it, Grandpa Frank had taught me many valuable lessons. I have even wondered on occasion if he knew exactly what he was doing in challenging my faith. One thing I am sure of, even if my Grandfather Farnsworth wasn't trying to purposely bless my life by giving me opposition, my Father in Heaven certainly was! I'm convinced that I wouldn't be in the profession that I am today if it hadn't been for the influence of my grandfather.

The Apostle Paul wrote to the Saints living in Corinth, "For there must be also heresies among you, that they which are approved may be made manifest among you" (1 Corinthians 11:19). My grandfather's attacks on my faith served as important opportunities for me to clarify and strengthen my testimony. The Prophet Joseph Smith taught, "by proving contraries, truth is made manifest."[12]

While I know my Grandfather Farnsworth will have to

make an accounting before the Lord for his opposition to the gospel, I look forward to seeing him again and resuming our relationship. I am forever grateful for the lessons I learned while doing battle with him.

Opposition is an important part of the Lord's plan as it helps us become who the Lord would have us be. Each of us has been created in the image and likeness of our heavenly parents and have been placed on earth as a means of learning to become gods ourselves. We have been blessed with the ability to reason and to receive revelation in answering the various challenges of life with which we are confronted each day. Our Heavenly Father wants us to be happy, but understands that happiness can only be experienced and understood in relation to sorrow. The Lord allows the subtleties of Satan and philosophies of men to exist as ways of teaching us his truths.

NOTES

1. Ezra Taft Benson, *The Teachings of Ezra Taft Benson* (Salt Lake City: Bookcraft, 1988), p. 56.

2. Brigham Young, as reported in James S. Brown, *Giant of the Lord* (Salt Lake City: Bookcraft, 1960), pp. 133–34.

3. Definitions adapted from Noah Webster, *American Dictionary of the English Language* (San Francisco: Foundation for American Christian Education, 1989).

4. Spencer W. Kimball, "The False Gods We Worship," *Ensign*, June 1976, p. 4.

5. Neal A. Maxwell, "Insights," *New Era*, April 1978, p. 6.

6. Harold B. Lee, in Conference Report, October 1950, p. 129.

7. Bruce R. McConkie, *The Millennial Messiah* (Salt Lake City: Deseret Book Co., 1982), p. 48.

8. Harold B. Lee, p. 131.

9. Richard G. Scott, "Healing the Tragic Scars of Abuse," *Ensign*, May 1992, p. 33.

10. This quotation is a variation of a statement originally made by Brigham Young: "We have the Gospel of life and salvation, to make bad men good and good men better" (in *Journal of Discourses*, 8:130). President David O. McKay is also credited with a similar statement.

11. Boyd K. Packer "The Mantle Is Far, Far Greater than the Intellect," *Charge to Religious Educators,* 2nd ed. (Salt Lake City: The Church of Jesus Christ of Latter-day Saints, 1982), p. 32.

12. Joseph Smith, in *History of the Church,* 6:48.

SECTION TWO

The Fall

5

Adam fell that men might be; and men are,
that they might have joy.
—2 Nephi 2:25

THE FALL OF ADAM, EVE,
AND ALL MANKIND

Most of the traditional Christian world believes that we (mankind) inherited an evil, sinful nature from Adam and Eve because of their partaking of the forbidden fruit in the Garden of Eden.[1] Consequently, from this traditional perspective, our evil desires and actions are direct results of this original sin. Because of this teaching, many Christians are led to view Adam and Eve with disdain, thinking that if they had not partaken of the forbidden fruit, we would not be plagued by our sinful, carnal natures, but be living in a state of peace and prosperity in the Garden of Eden. These ideas, which permeate the great majority of Christianity, are simply false. As we will discuss later, the doctrine of the Fall, when taught in this manner, becomes an excuse for sin.

The Restoration View of the Fall

Being all-knowing, God understands that for us to become like him we must develop our divine attributes in the same manner in which he did. We must come to an earth and experience growth through opposition. The Book of Mormon prophet Lehi taught his son Jacob this truth in the following: "And to bring about his eternal purposes in the end of man, after he had created our first parents, and the beasts of the field and the fowls of the air, and in fine, all things which are created, *it must needs be that there was an opposition;* even the forbidden fruit in opposition to the tree of life; the one being sweet and the other bitter" (2 Nephi 2:15; emphasis added).

Referring specifically to the inevitable opposition each of us faces in marriage and family relationships, President Gordon B. Hinckley has stated:

> Of course, all in marriage is not bliss. Years ago I clipped these words from a column written by Jenkins Lloyd Jones:
>
> "There seems to be a superstition among many thousands of our young who hold hands and smooch in the drive-ins that marriage is a cottage surrounded by perpetual hollyhocks to which a perpetually young and handsome husband comes home to a perpetually young and ravishing wife. When the hollyhocks wither and boredom and bills appear the divorce courts are jammed. . . .
>
> "Anyone who imagines that bliss is normal is going to waste a lot of time running around shouting that he has been robbed." (*Deseret News,* 12 June 1973, p. A4.)
>
> Stormy weather occasionally hits every household. Connected inevitably with the whole process is much of pain—physical, mental, and emotional. There is much of stress and struggle, of fear and worry. For most, there is the ever-haunting battle of economics. There seems never to be enough money to cover the needs of a family. Sickness strikes periodically. Accidents happen. The hand of death may reach in with dread stealth to take a precious one.
>
> But all of this seems to be part of the processes of family life. Few indeed are those who get along without experiencing some of it. It has been so from the beginning.[2]

In order to experience righteousness and joy, there must be the possibility of sin and misery. The very purpose behind the Lord placing the tree of knowledge of good and evil and the tree of life in the same garden was that Adam and Eve might learn to exercise their agency: "Wherefore, the Lord God gave unto man that he should act for himself. Wherefore, man could not act for himself save it should be that he was enticed by the one or the other." (2 Nephi 2:16.)

While some espouse the notion that we would be in a state of happiness if Adam and Eve had not partaken of the fruit, the prophet Lehi teaches us the truth of the matter. "If Adam had not transgressed he would not have fallen, but would have remained in the garden of Eden. . . . And they [Adam and Eve] would have had no children; wherefore they would have remained in a state of innocence, having no joy for they knew no misery; doing no good, for they knew no sin. But behold, all things have been done in the wisdom of him who knoweth all things. Adam fell that men might be; and men are, that they might have joy." (2 Nephi 2:22–25.) These verses are central to the doctrine of the Fall, but we often hear only the portion of the last sentence which states, "men are, that they might have joy." We miss an important portion of the text which explains that joy is only possible within the context of the Fall. *"Adam fell that men might be;* and men are, that they might have joy" (emphasis added).

Just as many Christians bemoan the fall of Adam and Eve, many of us lament the fact that we too have to experience the bitter to comprehend the sweet. The couple I spoke of in the preface to this book (the Carters) resented the fact that their relationship wasn't in the same state of "creation" as it had been during their early days of courtship and marriage. The reality of children, finances, Church assignments, sickness, and job-related pressures had replaced the relative innocence and simplicity they had once shared. They didn't understand the doctrine that in order for us to comprehend joy "it must needs be, that there is an opposition in all things" (2 Nephi 2:11).

When many of us experience opposition we respond with feelings of resentment toward our spouses, families, jobs, or other life circumstances. Some of us blame Adam for our woes, others Eve. Still others blame our mothers and/or fathers, some women blame Mars and some men Venus. Many of us are convinced that our problems are caused by our spouses, our children, the boss, secret combinations, and some of us even eclipse the truth by blaming ourselves. The only thing blame brings is bitterness, and it serves as a self-deceptive logic for not moving forward. To place blame on anyone or anything is to wrongly recast the characters and rewrite the script for the initial drama of life that began in the Garden of Eden. To blame another is a legitimized doctrine of the devil, whether our resentment is focused on Adam and Eve, Mom and Dad, or even the devil himself. Elder James E. Talmage wrote:

> It has become a common practise with mankind to heap reproaches upon the progenitors of the family, and to picture the supposedly blessed state in which we would be living but for the fall; whereas our first parents are entitled to our deepest gratitude for their legacy to posterity—the means of winning title to glory, exaltation, and eternal lives. But for the opportunity thus given, the spirits of God's offspring would have remained forever in a state of innocent childhood, sinless through no effort of their own; negatively saved, not from sin, but from the opportunity of meeting sin; incapable of winning the honors of victory because [they were] prevented from taking part in the conflict. As it is, they are heirs to the birthright of Adam's descendants—mortality, with its immeasurable possibilities and its God-given freedom of action. From Father Adam we have inherited all the ills to which flesh is heir; but such are necessarily incident to a knowledge of good and evil, by the proper use of which knowledge man may become even as the Gods.[3]

Beginning with a distorted understanding of the fall of Adam and Eve, many people have come to believe and teach that we would be in a state of peace and prosperity if our parents hadn't been alcoholic, abusive, emotionally distant, or enmeshed. Influenced by these ideas, many of us have grown up with the idea that our problems are the result of our environment. In other words, we come to believe that our problems are always someone else's or something else's fault. We deny individual responsibility and accountability for our problems and solutions. Sadly, by blaming our circumstances for our problems we also give up any real hope for peace. For in thinking this way, our happiness is dependent upon circumstances which may be largely, or even completely, out of our control. This isn't to say that the fall of Adam and Eve, the sins of our parents, or other difficult circumstances of life don't influence us and bring us pain; they have, they do, and they will, but these circumstances need not make us evil or ruin our lives. The fall of Adam and Eve as well as the fall of all mankind has significant meaning to each of us, as it brought opposition, which is an essential part of the very purpose of our earthly existence. Mortality, with its accompanying challenges and our own personal weaknesses, provides opportunities for growth that we couldn't experience any other way.

Some of us attempt to solve our problems by changing our environment. We falsely believe that a divorce, job change, or other change in our circumstances will bring the happiness we seek. The scriptures plainly teach, however, that regardless of circumstance, "he that is happy shall be happy still; and he that is unhappy shall be unhappy still" (Mormon 9:14). Hopefully, we will eventually come to the realization that even though our spouse, job, or other circumstances may have changed, our problems remain the same. The changes that need to come about are not in our circumstances, but in our hearts. Note the following words from President Ezra Taft Benson. "The Lord works from the inside out. The world works from the outside in. The world would take people out of the slums. Christ takes the slums out of people, and then they take themselves out of the slums. The world would mold men by changing their environment. Christ changes men, who then change their environment. The world would shape human behavior, but Christ can change human nature."[4]

The scriptures clearly teach that the possibility of personal sin and misery must have existed for Adam and Eve and for each of us if we could ever hope to experience righteousness and joy. One cannot have one without the other, they are "a compound in one" (2 Nephi 2:11).

The fall of Adam and Eve introduced spiritual and physical death into the world. Spiritual death in the sense that Adam and Eve were no longer in the presence of God, and physical death in that their immortal bodies became mortal—subject to weakness and, eventually, death. However, through the atonement of Jesus Christ all mankind has been redeemed from the fall of Adam and Eve and is free from the effects of their transgression. "Yea, behold, this death bringeth to pass the resurrection, and redeemeth all mankind from the first death—that spiritual death; for all mankind, by the fall of Adam being cut off from the presence of the Lord, are considered as dead, both as to things temporal and to things spiritual. But behold, the resurrection of Christ redeemeth mankind, yea, even all mankind, and bringeth them back into the presence of the Lord." (Helaman 14:16–17.) Everything that is lost in the fall of Adam and Eve is regained in the atonement of Christ. Not only does the Atonement guarantee that all will be resurrected, this infinite act also insures that everyone will be brought back into the presence of God (see Helaman 14:17). For some, being in God's presence will only be for a short period of judgment before they leave to inhabit a lesser kingdom. For others it will be their privilege not only to be in God's presence for judgment, but to dwell with him eternally.

The Atonement also extends back to our premortal lives. The scriptures teach that even though we exercised our agency in the premortal life and rose to greater or lesser levels of nobility (see Abraham 3:22), we were born into this mortal world neither good nor evil, but *innocent*. "Every spirit of man was innocent in the beginning; and God having redeemed man from the fall, men became again, in their infant state, innocent before God" (D&C 93:38). From the age of accountability, we pass beyond innocence and begin to be accountable for our own natures as a consequence of exercising our moral agency to choose between good and evil. The scriptures also teach that the influence of the adversary and the traditions of our fathers play a part in defining who we are. "And that wicked one cometh and taketh away light and truth, through disobedience, from the children of men, and because of the tradition of their fathers" (D&C 93:39).

The question is sometimes asked, what about those who grow up in hellish environments—are they responsible for their actions? The prophet Mormon taught: "For behold, the Spirit of Christ is given to *every man*, that he may know good from evil" (Moroni 7:16; emphasis added). Each of us is accountable to a greater or lesser degree for the light and knowledge we have been given. The Lord states in the Doctrine and Covenants "he who sins against the greater light shall receive the greater condemnation" (D&C 82:3). We can also conclude from this verse that he who sins against the lesser light shall receive the lesser condemnation. This point of doctrine could account for why we see some of the happiest and some of the saddest marriages and families among the Latter-day Saints.

While it isn't a popular doctrine, especially in our day, the Lord has taught that each of us is accountable and responsible for our own lives. Samuel the Lamanite taught: "And now remember, remember, my brethren, that whosoever perisheth, perisheth unto himself; and whosoever doeth iniquity, doeth it unto himself; for behold, ye are free; ye are permitted to act for yourselves; for behold, God hath given unto you a knowledge and he hath made you free. He hath given unto you that ye might know good from evil, and he hath given unto you that ye might choose life or death." (Helaman 14:30–31.) However, not only is God a God of justice he is a God of mercy as well. President J. Reuben Clark once taught, "I feel that [the Savior] will give that punishment which is the very least that our transgression will justify. . . . When it comes to making the rewards for our good conduct, he will give us the maximum that it is possible to give."[5] It is comforting to know that God is, and will always be, perfectly merciful and perfectly just in his judgments of each of us.

It is also important to point out that we can suffer the consequences of breaking the commandments by transgressing the law unknowingly (see Mosiah 3:11). Consider the following illustration. For example's sake, let's say that I invited you to my home for supper. Upon entering our home, my youngest son, Adam, provides you with a glass of punch. Being thirsty (and wanting to be polite), you consume the beverage and are invited to have some more. During the course of the evening you end up having consumed four large glasses of punch. Unknown to you (and Adam), I have spiked the punch with alcohol! Have you sinned by partaking of the alcohol? Of course the answer is no, but even though you are not morally accountable for what you have done, you will still suffer the consequences of drinking the alcohol, for in one sense you have transgressed the law—you have taken alcohol into your body.

It is also possible to suffer the consequences of sin when the sins that are committed are not our own. I have worked with many individuals who have been physically, sexually, or emotionally abused. In many cases these individuals have literally suffered "the iniquity of their fathers" (Numbers 14:18). Elder Richard G. Scott has stated the following concerning the accountability of those involved in such situations: "I solemnly testify that when another's acts of violence, perversion, or incest hurt you terribly, against your will, you are not responsible and you must not feel guilty. You may be left scarred by abuse, but those scars need not be permanent. In the eternal plan, in the Lord's timetable, those injuries can be made right as you do your part."[6]

One of the most profound truths that these abuse victims have taught me is that as terrible as the abuse is, it is not the act of the abuser that has the power to ruin their lives; happiness or misery is found in the response of the abused. In my experience, those who have successfully worked through the implications of this kind of abuse have eventually come to the same conclusion: "There is nothing from without a man, that entering into him can defile him: but the things which come out of him, those are they that defile the man" (Mark 7:15). Note the following example of this truth in the words of one of my former students, Laura:

As a child I was abused by my older brother. At the time I knew what my brother did was wrong, yet I still loved him. As I grew older, however, I learned to hate him. As I came face to face with the everyday problems of life, I didn't accept the responsibility for my own mistakes and faults. I looked for an excuse—a way out. I looked for someone or something else to blame. I began having problems with my physical health, but when I began to get well I refused to accept it. I didn't want to return to the everyday problems that would be waiting for me. That was when the hate for my brother really grew. In my mind, all of my problems were his fault. I realize now, it was then that it became my sin. My hate, my anger was what hurt me—it made me sick. The hate for my own brother had grown so strong and fierce that it left him behind. I hated myself, my family, my friends, this earth, and its creator. I think that when you hate everyone the void is so powerful that if you don't find love, if you don't give love, you die. That's where the gospel came in. That was when I finally realized there was something more to life than my bitterness. Being part of the Church had never really been important to me. It became worthless, because I didn't do my part. So I began for the first time to work, to really live the gospel. I found that in return Heavenly Father began to give more to me than anything I could ever give him. My happiness and peace became his gift to me. With each day of my life as I give all that I can give, I can't even comprehend the blessings he gives me.[7]

Laura eventually came to understand that her problems had more to do with what she was doing in response to the abuse than what had been done to her by her abuser. Sadly, she had been taught by her therapist that her recovery would progress in direct proportion to the amount of anger she was able to express toward her brother. A majority of Laura's "therapy" focused on instructing her on various ways to "get in touch" with her hatred for her brother and then learn to express it. Gratefully, Laura listened to her wise and kind bishop. While not having any professional training as a psychologist, Laura's bishop knew the gospel of Jesus Christ well enough to tell

Laura that what she was being taught by her therapist was wrong. Instead of encouraging her to hate her enemy, he encouraged her to love her brother: "Ye have heard that it hath been said, Thou shalt love thy neighbour, and hate thine enemy. But I say unto you, Love your enemies, bless them that curse you, do good to them that hate you, and pray for them which despitefully use you, and persecute you." (Matthew 5:43–44.)

The Savior also said, "resist not evil: but whosoever shall smite thee on thy right cheek, turn to him the other also" (Matthew 5:39). This shouldn't be understood as the Savior counseling us to encourage or even allow others to continue to abuse us, but for us not to revile against them and exchange "evil for evil" (Romans 12:17). This teaching is clarified in the following text from the Joseph Smith Translation of Luke:

> But I say unto you who hear my words, Love your enemies, do good to them who hate you.
>
> Bless them who curse you, and pray for them who despitefully use you and persecute you.
>
> And unto him who smiteth thee on the cheek, offer also the other; or, in other words, *it is better to offer the other, than to revile again.* And him who taketh away thy cloak, forbid not to take thy coat also.
>
> For it is better that thou suffer thine enemy to take these things, than to contend with him. Verily I say unto you, Your heavenly Father who seeth in secret, shall bring that wicked one into judgment. (JST, Luke 6:27–30; emphasis added.)

President Kimball taught: "Sometimes the spirit of forgiveness is carried to the loftiest height—to rendering assistance to the offender. Not to be revengeful, not to seek what outraged justice might demand, to leave the offender in God's hands—this is admirable. But to return good for evil, this is the sublime expression of Christian love."[8] Laura was eventually able to let go of her hatred and forgive her brother. She also came to understand the necessity of repenting of the hate she held for him. It is also important to acknowledge the fact that Laura's forgiveness of her brother included a willingness to share her story with legal authorities as well as her Church leaders (see D&C 42:84–89). But instead of wanting to punish her abuser for what he had done, she sincerely wanted to help him repent of his actions. Laura came to understand that truly loving someone includes both justice *and* mercy.

I offer a silent prayer of praise and thanks every time I hear from Laura. Today, she is a valiant, dedicated member of the Church who is striving to understand the gospel and live it to the best of her ability. She no longer suffers from the depression and suicidal thoughts that once consumed her life. Laura's story is a modern-day miracle.

Just as Laura learned that her problems weren't all her brother's fault, so must we learn that it is our own sins and not Adam's transgression that bring about our sinful natures. The following verses clarify this doctrine by teaching that Adam's and Eve's children acquired their own sinful natures as a consequence of their own sins and not their parents' transgression: "And Adam and Eve blessed the name of God, and they made all things known unto their sons and daughters. And Satan came among them, saying: I am a son of God; and he commanded them, saying: Believe it not; and they believed it not and they loved Satan more than God. And men began *from that time forth* to be carnal, sensual, and devilish." (Moses 5:12–13; emphasis added. See also D&C 20:20; Articles of Faith 1:2.)

Just as most Christianity places the blame for our fallen condition on our first parents (Adam and Eve), many people see their problems as being caused by someone or something else. Also, many social scientists and practitioners place the blame for our existing problems on our "dysfunctional family"—namely our mothers and fathers. Sigmund Freud taught that our personalities are formed at an early age in direct response to early childhood experiences, particularly the influence of our parents. Freud and his followers maintain that later in life, our tendencies to think, feel, and behave in the ways in which we do are *determined* by these early factors. From this principle follows the notion that we are not responsible for being the way that we are; our personalities are the psychic product of the way in which our parents raised us. From a Freudian perspective, the best that we can expect is insight into this cause-and-effect process and the ability to learn to cope with it.

Secular Philosophy and the Nature of Man

Even though there are many semantical and practical differences between the different psychological theories and therapies, many share the common theme that our personalities are determined by forces beyond our agency. These theories embody the idea that we are either the victim or the beneficiary of our environment, whether that environment be physical, emotional, mental, or biochemical.

As we discussed earlier, many psychologists, psychiatrists, and social workers teach that we would be in a state of peace and prosperity if our parents hadn't been alcoholic, abusive, emotionally distant, or enmeshed. Influenced by these ideas, many of us have grown up with the idea that our problems are the result of our environment. In other words, our problems are always someone else's or something else's fault. We deny individual responsibility and accountability for our problems. Interestingly enough, by blaming our circumstances for our problems we also give up any real hope for peace. For in thinking this way, our happiness is dependent upon circumstances which may be largely out of our control. This isn't to say that the fall of Adam and Eve, the sins of our parents, or our circumstances in general haven't influenced us; they have, but they haven't made us evil nor need they ruin our lives.

The fall of both sets of our parents has significant meaning to each of us as to the very purpose of our earthly existence. Mortality and its accompanying challenges as well as our own weaknesses provide an opportunity for growth that we couldn't experience in any other way.

I have always been interested in the scriptural account of Joseph (Jacob's son) concerning the abuse that he received at the hands of his own brothers:

> And when Joseph's brethren saw that their father was dead, they said, Joseph will peradventure hate us, and will certainly requite us all the evil which we did unto him.
>
> And they sent a messenger unto Joseph, saying, Thy father did command before he died, saying,
>
> So shall ye say unto Joseph, Forgive, I pray thee now, the trespass of thy brethren, and their sin; for they did unto thee evil: and now, we pray thee, forgive the trespass of the servants of the God of thy father. And Joseph wept when they spake unto him.
>
> And his brethren also went and fell down before his face; and they said, Behold, we be thy servants.
>
> And Joseph said unto them, Fear not: for am I in the place of God?
>
> But as for you, ye thought evil against me; but God meant it unto good, to bring to pass, as it is this day, to save much people alive.
>
> Now therefore fear ye not: I will nourish you, and your little ones. And he comforted them, and spake kindly unto them. (Genesis 50:15–21; see also D&C 100:15.)

The Lord has said that the evil and adversity we face is an essential part of knowing him and becoming like him: "That ye may be the children of your Father which is in heaven: for he maketh his sun to rise on the evil and on the good, and sendeth rain on the just and on the unjust" (Matthew 5:45).

President Spencer W. Kimball has stated:

> Is there not wisdom in giving us trials that we might rise above them, responsibilities that we might achieve, work to harden our muscles, sorrows to try our souls? Are we not exposed to temptations to test our strength, sickness that we might learn patience, death that we might be immortalized and glorified?

If all the sick for whom we pray were healed, if all the righteous were protected and the wicked destroyed, the whole program of the Father would be annulled and the basic principle of the gospel, free agency, would be ended. No man would have to live by faith.

If joy and peace and rewards were instantaneously given the doer of good, there could be no evil—all would do good but not because of the rightness of doing good. There would be no test of strength, no development of character, no growth of powers, no free agency, only satanic controls.

Should all prayers be immediately answered according to our selfish desires and our limited understanding, then there would be little or no suffering, sorrow, disappointment, or even death, and if these were not, there would also be no joy, success, resurrection, nor eternal life and godhood.[9]

The great lesson to be learned from the doctrine of the Fall is that there is purpose in opposition. Joy can be fully experienced only in the context of sorrow; without hell there could be no heaven. Mother Eve wisely taught, "Were it not for our transgression we . . . never should have known good and evil, and the joy of our redemption, and the eternal life which God giveth unto all the obedient" (Moses 5:11).

NOTES

1. See LaMar Garrard, "The Fall of Man," in *Principles of the Gospel in Practice* (Salt Lake City: Randall Books, 1985), pp. 39–70.

2. Gordon B. Hinckley, "What God Hath Joined Together," *Ensign,* May 1991, p. 72.

3. James E. Talmage, *The Articles of Faith,* 12 ed. (Salt Lake City: The Church of Jesus Christ of Latter-day Saints, 1977), p. 70.

4. Ezra Taft Benson, "Born of God," *Ensign,* November 1985, p. 6.

5. J. Reuben Clark, "As Ye Sow . . . ," *Brigham Young University Speeches of the Year* (Provo: BYU, 1955), p. 7. As cited by Elder Vaughn J. Featherstone, " 'Forgive Them, I Pray Thee,' " *Ensign,* November 1980, p. 31.

6. Richard G. Scott, "Healing the Tragic Scars of Abuse," *Ensign*, May 1992, p. 32.

7. Account originally published in Daniel K Judd, "The Doctrines of Submission and Forgiveness," in *Doctrines for Exaltation, the 1989 Sperry Symposium on the Doctrine and Covenants* (Salt Lake City: Deseret Book Co., 1989), p. 124.

8. Spencer W. Kimball, *The Miracle of Forgiveness* (Salt Lake City: Bookcraft, 1969), p. 284.

9. Spencer W. Kimball, *Faith Precedes the Miracle* (Salt Lake City: Deseret Book Co., 1972), p. 97.

6

Therefore to him that knoweth to do good,
and doeth it not, to him it is sin.
—James 4:17

WHAT EVER BECAME OF SIN?

While a portion of the suffering and opposition we face in life comes to us by no fault of our own, the scriptures and our modern prophets have taught that the most persistent cause of suffering is our own personal violation of the commandments of God. Note the words of President Spencer W. Kimball:

> There are many causes for human suffering—including war, disease, and poverty—and the suffering that proceeds from each of these is very real, but I would not be true to my trust if I did not say that the most persistent cause of human suffering, that suffering which causes the deepest pain, is sin— the violation of the commandments given to us by God. There cannot be, for instance, a rich and full life unless we practice total chastity before marriage and total fidelity after. There cannot be a sense of wholeness and integrity if we lie, steal, or cheat. There cannot be sweetness in our lives if we are filled with envy or covetousness. Our lives cannot really be abundant if we do not honor our parents.[1]

Professor C. Terry Warner's work regarding self-betrayal has been essential in the writing of this chapter. This chapter is my brief expression of some of the ideas found in *Bonds of Anguish, Bonds of Love.* See also Brother Warner's, "Repenting of Unrighteous Feelings," a Ricks College Devotional address given 1 March 1983.

Such a simple doctrine, sin, but the doctrine of sin has nearly been lost from our culture. We seemed to have replaced sin with words like *mistake* and *error,* which lessen the degree of personal responsibility for our actions. In the book of James we read the following definition, "Therefore to him that knoweth to do good, and doeth it not, to him it is sin" (James 4:17; see also Romans 7:7; 2 Nephi 9:25).

Many of us have the mistaken idea that to really be guilty of sin we must commit some grave act like murder or adultery. While these acts are certainly two of the most serious sins, there are other sins which may be considered less serious, but in time, can bring similar results. In the Book of Mormon we read: "And there shall also be many which shall say: Eat, drink, and be merry; nevertheless, fear God—he will justify in committing a little sin; . . . there is no harm in this; . . . and if it so be that we are guilty, God will beat us with a few stripes, and at last we shall be saved in the kingdom of God. . . . And thus the devil cheateth their souls, and leadeth them away carefully down to hell." (2 Nephi 28:8, 21.)

God is a God of mercy, but he is not a God of indulgence. We know that "no unclean thing can enter into his kingdom" (3 Nephi 27:19) and that any sin, no matter how small, disqualifies us from entering his presence. C. S. Lewis provided profound insight as to how the adversary uses small sins to lead us to greater ones. In his fictional book, *The Screwtape Letters,* C. S. Lewis's master devil, Screwtape, instructs his apprentice devil Wormwood on the power of simple sins:

> You will say that these are very small sins; and doubtless, like all young tempters, you are anxious to be able to report spectacular wickedness. But do remember, the only thing that matters is the extent you separate the man from the enemy. It does not matter how small the sins are, provided that their cumulative effect is to edge the man away from the Light and out into the Nothing. Murder is no better than cards if cards can do the trick. Indeed, the safest road to Hell is the gradual one—the gentle slope, soft underfoot, without sudden turnings, without milestones, without signposts.[2]

When we were first married, my wife and I made an agreement that we would never watch an R-rated movie. While on occasion we watch PG-13 movies with our children, we have usually waited to watch them after our children have gone to bed. We have reasoned that while the content of these movies wasn't suitable for young people, as adults we had the maturity to watch them without being harmed. Imagine my feelings when I read the following words from Elder J. Richard Clarke: "Any film, television show, music, or printed material unfit for youth is also unfit for parents. Those who rationalize acceptance of immoral material on grounds of maturity or sophistication are deceived."[3]

When I read Elder Clarke's words, I knew what he was saying was right. In fact, I knew his words were true even before I read them, because every time I had watched a movie after having tucked my children into bed, I had to rationalize why doing so was okay. The very presence of my rationalizations indicated that I knew what I was doing was wrong. Besides using the justification that my wife and I were mature enough to watch such material without being adversely affected, I had also used other rationalizations such as:

> 1) "How could watching such a movie be so bad, it won an Academy Award."
> 2) "I need to stay current by being aware of what the public is watching."
> 3) "What's the big deal, everyone else watches R-rated movies!"
> 4) "All G-rated movies are simplistic, I want to watch something intellectually challenging."
> 5) "It's better my children are in bed, they wouldn't understand it anyway."

In order to go against my conscience and still feel good about myself, I had to talk myself into believing my own lie. What makes our rationalizations so powerful is that in making them we eclipse ourselves from the truth and come to actually believe what we are doing (or not doing) is right. John the Beloved taught, "If we say we have no sin, we deceive ourselves, and the truth is not in us" (1 John 1:8).

While it may seem extreme to label my watching a PG-13 movie without my children as sinful, that is exactly what it was. To paraphrase the Apostle James, I knew to do good and did it not, therefore to me it was sin. Even though my rationalizations were logical and would be supported by most people, they were immoral because they were personal justifications that allowed me not to be true to what I knew to be right. Sins, large and small, truly are the cause of most of the problems we face.

The Sin of Self-righteousness

Not all sins are as simple to see as my example with the movies. In the fall of 1979 I asked Kaye Seegmiller to become my wife. Her acceptance of my proposal was one of the most important days of my life. While I knew Kaye's parents didn't know me well and were somewhat cautious about her marrying me, I was totally dumbfounded by their response when we called them on the phone and informed them of our marriage plans. After Kaye had said, "Hi, Mom and Dad, I'm getting married!" one of them responded by saying, "Who to?" I took offense as I listened to Kaye and her parents discuss her decision to marry me and not the missionary she had waited for. I couldn't believe that they weren't thrilled to have me as a son-in-law. My parents would be supportive, why couldn't Kaye's parents feel the same way? I justified my resentment towards Kaye's parents by judging them as being insensitive and unkind. Sensing them to be unsupportive of our plans, I asked if I could speak to Kaye's father on the phone privately. After Kaye and her mother were off the phone, I informed Brother Seegmiller, in what I felt to be a very controlled and courageous manner, that Kaye and I were going to get married on December 28th and would appreciate their support. I didn't say it, but I was certainly implying that we would go ahead with the wedding whether they were supportive or not! The conversation ended, and instead of celebrating a joyous occasion, Kaye was in tears and I was angry—not quite the way I had wanted our engagement to begin.

While Kaye's parents quickly accepted the fact that we were getting married and fully supported us throughout our engagement and marriage, I held on to the resentment that I had felt the night of our phone conversation. As the next few years began to unfold, I looked for every reason possible not to spend time with Kaye's parents and family. I didn't feel accepted by them and didn't want to deal with those feelings any more than I had to. When we did go to their home, I made sure I had other things to do while I was there. I had decided that in-laws really were as difficult as all the jokes about them said they were.

How should I have dealth with this situation? Some people (even some therapists) would have had me be "honest about my feelings" and express the resentment I had toward my in-laws. Others would pat me on the back and praise me for being able to be in such control of my "righteous indignation." I had taken the control route because I had thought it to be the more righteous choice.[4] I interpreted Paul's words, "Be ye angry, and sin not" (Ephesians 4:26) to mean that it was okay to be angry as long as I was in control.

Let's read the Savior's words regarding individuals whose attitudes were similar to my own: "Woe unto you, scribes and Pharisees, hypocrites! for ye are like unto whited sepulchers, which indeed appear beautiful outward, but are within full of dead men's bones, and of all uncleanness. Even so ye also outwardly appear righteous unto men, but within ye are full of hypocrisy and iniquity." (Matthew 23:27–28.)

While there is much controversy in the world (and among Church members) regarding the control or expression of anger, I have found the scriptures to be quite specific on the subject. Note the following comparison of the Bible with the Book of Mormon, with respect to anger. From the King James Version of the New Testament we read:

Ye have heard that it was said by them of old time, Thou shalt not kill; and whosoever shall kill shall be in danger of the judgment:

But I say unto you, That whosoever is angry with his brother *without a cause* shall be in danger of the judgment: and whosoever shall say to his brother, Raca, shall be in danger of the council: but whosoever shall say, Thou fool, shall be in danger of hell fire (Matthew 5:21–22; emphasis added).

The Book of Mormon and the Joseph Smith Translation of the Bible read this way:

Ye have heard that it hath been said by them of old time, and it is also written before you, that thou shalt not kill, and whosoever shall kill shall be in danger of the judgment of God;

But I say unto you, that whosoever is angry with his brother shall be in danger of his judgment. And whosoever shall say to his brother, Raca, shall be in danger of the council; and whosoever shall say, Thou fool, shall be in danger of hell fire. (3 Nephi 12:21–22; see also JST, Matthew 5:23–24.)

A careful comparison of these two texts reveals that the phrase "without a cause" does not appear in either the Book of Mormon or the Joseph Smith Translation of the Bible! The implication of this difference is significant as the biblical translation appears to provide justification for our anger, the Book of Mormon and the Joseph Smith Translation of the Bible do not.

It is interesting to note that while the King James Version contains the phrase "without a cause," most biblical translations do not. One biblical scholar has written that while there isn't a unanimous consensus among the early manuscripts, many of the early Christian theologians such as Jerome, Tertullian, and Origen mention that the phrase "without a cause" was not found in the oldest manuscripts familiar to them.[5]

Note another comparison of the King James Version and the Joseph Smith Translation of the Bible with respect to Paul's teachings on anger:

Be ye angry, and sin not: let not the sun go down upon your wrath (Ephesians 4:26).

Can ye be angry, and not sin? let not the sun go down upon your wrath (JST, Ephesians 4:26).

Again, the King James Version of the Bible appears to justify anger, the Joseph Smith Translation invites us to judge for ourselves. The prophet Nephi describes his struggles with anger in the following:

And why should I yield to sin, because of my flesh? Yea, why should I give way to temptations, that the evil one have place in my heart to destroy my peace and afflict my soul? Why am I angry because of mine enemy?

Awake, my soul! No longer droop in sin. Rejoice, O my heart, and give place no more for the enemy of my soul.

Do not anger again because of mine enemies. Do not slacken my strength because of mine afflictions.

Rejoice, O my heart, and cry unto the Lord, and say: O Lord, I will praise thee forever; yea, my soul will rejoice in thee, my God, and the rock of my salvation. (2 Nephi 4:27–30.)

While it is clear that the Book of Mormon contains strong teachings against anger, how are we to understand the anger of righteous men such as Moroni (see Alma 59:13) or even the anger of God himself (see Helaman 13:11)? One is led to ask the question, "Isn't there such an experience as righteous anger?" One might also question, "What of the incidences in the scriptures where the Savior was angry—aren't we to follow his example?"

An analysis of the Bible shows that the Old Testament contains 375 instances where God is described as being angry.*

---

* A computer analysis of the Old Testament revealed that the Hebrew word for anger ('aph {af}) appears 455 times out of which 375 times it is referring to the anger of the Lord. There are 42 instances of the Lord's anger in the Book of Mormon (150 total instances of a form of the word *anger*).

Surprisingly, the New Testament has only one reference where the word anger is used in connection with Jesus Christ:

> And he [Jesus] entered again into the synagogue; and there was a man there which had a withered hand.
>
> And they [the Pharisees] watched him, whether he would heal him on the sabbath day; that they might accuse him.
>
> And he saith unto the man which had the withered hand, Stand forth.
>
> And he saith unto them, Is it lawful to do good on the sabbath days, or to do evil? to save life, or to kill? But they held their peace.
>
> And when he [Jesus] had looked round about on them [the Pharisees] with *anger, being grieved for the hardness of their hearts,* he saith unto the man, Stretch forth thine hand. And he stretched it out: and his hand was restored whole as the other.
>
> And the Pharisees went forth, and straightway took counsel with the Herodians against him, how they might destroy him. (Mark 3:1–6; emphasis added.)

From the above text, it is apparent that the Savior's anger was a selfless concern not only for the man with the withered hand, but for the hard-heartedness of the Pharisees as well. One of the things we can learn from this account is that the Savior's anger is fundamentally different than the anger of the natural man. Most everything the natural man does is calculated in some way to "[serve] the creature more than the Creator" (Romans 1:25), while the Book of Mormon teaches us that everything the Savior does is designed for the welfare and happiness of others. "He doeth not *anything* save it be for the benefit of the world; for he loveth the world, even that he layeth down his own life that he may draw all men unto him. Wherefore, he commandeth none that they shall not partake of his salvation." (2 Nephi 26:24; emphasis added.)

The Book of Mormon also teaches us that the Savior's anger is a representation of his love for us. Justice is as much a quality of God's love as mercy.

Yea, and we may see at the very time when he doth pros-
per his people, yea, in the increase of their fields, their flocks
and their herds, and in gold, and in silver, and in all manner of
precious things of every kind and art; sparing their lives, and
delivering them out of the hands of their enemies; softening
the hearts of their enemies that they should not declare wars
against them; yea, and in fine, *doing all things for the welfare
and happiness of his people;* yea, then is the time that they do
harden their hearts, and do forget the Lord their God, and do
trample under their feet the Holy One—yea, and this because
of their ease, and their exceedingly great prosperity.

And thus we see that *except the Lord doth chasten his people*
with many afflictions, yea, except he doth visit them with
death and with terror, and with famine and with all manner of
pestilence, they will not remember him. (Helaman 12:2–3;
emphasis added.)

God wants nothing more than for us to remember him and
keep his commandments, for in doing so we qualify for the
blessings of heaven and earth. God's anger is much like his jealousy; both are expressions of his omnipotent love as he seeks to
assist us in becoming like him. God's jealousy of our worship of
other gods isn't narcissistic in any way, but a plea that we remain free from the damning consequences of worshiping them:

Thou shalt not make unto thee any graven image, or any
likeness of any thing that is in heaven above, or that is in the
earth beneath, or that is in the water under the earth:

Thou shalt not bow down thyself to them, nor serve them:
for I the Lord thy God am a jealous God, visiting the iniquity
of the fathers upon the children unto the third and fourth
generation of them that hate me;

And shewing mercy unto thousands of them that love me,
and keep my commandments (Exodus 20:4–6).

Anger is indeed a characteristic of God's perfection, but it is
critical that we come to a *correct* understanding of his selfless
nature and seek to follow his example.

I eventually learned that the answer to the feelings of resentment I had toward my in-laws wasn't to be found in venting my anger nor in controlling it, but in denying myself "of all ungodliness" (Moroni 10:32) by repenting of my less than godly feelings. To my surprise, my father- and mother-in-law never had feelings of ill will toward me. Their only concern was the welfare of their daughter.

Looking Beyond the Mark (Perfectionism)

Another vice which masquerades as virtue, in which many of us participate, is commonly called perfectionism. One scriptural term that is related to this problem was described by the Book of Mormon prophet Jacob as "looking beyond the mark" (Jacob 4:14). Though there are several different manifestations of this way of living (recall the story of Esther in chapter two), the following example shows how this behavior is often acted out between husbands and wives.

Several years ago I received a phone call from a woman who asked if I could help her deal with some of the psychological problems she was facing that were associated with a chronic illness with which she was suffering.* As we talked it soon became quite evident that in addition to her physical and emotional health being in jeopardy, her marriage and family were in serious trouble as well. She related to me how disappointed she was in her husband's "faithlessness" in his Church responsibilities and how her oldest son was following his example. She described to me in great detail how the week before she had thought that maybe there was some hope for her husband. He had told her that he was going to take their fifteen-year-old son to the priesthood session of general conference only to find out later that they had gone to the shooting range instead. They had deliberately deceived her by walking out of the house dressed for the meeting, then changing into other clothes that

---

* Identifying information in this story has been changed to protect this family.

they had hidden in the pickup truck. They had then changed back into their dress clothes before coming home. She was quite sure that divorce was the only option as her husband was setting such a poor example for the children. She also described how he drank alcohol from time to time and was once involved with another woman. I asked if it was possible to meet with them as a couple. She said that she didn't want the three of us to meet together because her husband would just "twist things around" and make her look bad, but she reluctantly agreed to ask him. After several weeks of his wife insisting he meet with me, he finally agreed.

As anyone who has spent time talking to couples in conflict will appreciate, his side of the story was quite different from his wife's. His first question to me was to ask if I thought his wife would be helped by psychiatric hospitalization. He then asserted that he was married to a "religious fanatic." When I asked him about the incident where he and his son had gone shooting instead of to priesthood meeting, he agreed they probably shouldn't have deceived her, but that he had a good reason for doing what he did. He then related to me the events that had occurred earlier that Saturday as an example of what his wife was *really* like. She had insisted the entire family watch general conference on television from 10:00 A.M. to 12:00 noon and then again from 2:00 P.M. to 4:00 P.M. on Saturday. Not only had she insisted they all watch conference, she expected them to be dressed in their Sunday clothes and sit quietly through the sessions. He thought this was especially inappropriate for their younger children (three children under ten years of age), as well as their thirteen-year-old daughter, fifteen-year-old son, and him! He explained to me how he had tried to reason with her in the past, but she would typically become sullen and lock herself in the bedroom, later crying that he wasn't being supportive of rearing the children in the Church.

The husband further explained to me how his lack of devotion to religious matters was his attempt to balance his wife's fanatical religious behavior. He didn't want his children to grow up being religious fanatics like their mother. He reasoned that while he knew some of his actions seemed inappropriate, he was simply doing the best he could do under very difficult circumstances.

Interestingly, his wife would later explain to me how everything she was doing was meant only to save their children. She felt she wasn't being a fanatic, but trying to help her children learn to live the gospel in spite of the bad example of their father.

Do you see what was happening? Both the husband and the wife were seeing each other as the problem, and for years their solution had been to insist that the other one change. The wife wanted the husband to become more religious, the husband wanted the wife to be less fanatical. Also, each saw themselves as doing what they had to do to "save the children." In reality, they were in a downward spiral of blame and accusation that was not only destroying their marriage, but their relationships with their children as well. Can you see how the children in the family might even choose to become allies with either the father or the mother or disassociate themselves from the family all together? What would you say has to change for this troubled relationship to be healed?

First of all we must understand that whether our problems are with our spouses, our children, our neighbors, or business associates, "seeing other people as the problem is the problem."[6] This is part of what the Savior was teaching us when he said:

> Judge not, that ye be not judged.
>
> For with what judgment ye judge, ye shall be judged: and with what measure ye mete, it shall be measured to you again.
>
> And why beholdest thou the mote that is in thy brother's eye, but considerest not the beam that is in thine own eye?
>
> Or how wilt thou say to thy brother, Let me pull out the mote out of thine eye; and, behold, a beam is in thine own eye?
>
> Thou hypocrite, first cast out the beam out of thine own eye; and then shalt thou see clearly to cast out the mote out of thy brother's eye. (Matthew 7:1–5; see also JST, Matthew 7:1–2.)

The answer to solving this problem is found in the latter part of this passage, "first cast out the beam out of thine own eye." This was an extemely difficult principle for the wife in this case to understand. At first, she couldn't understand how doing all of the "righteous" things she had been doing could be part of the problem. After all, she was doing only what the scriptures and prophets had been teaching her! It wasn't until she came to understand the truth contained in the following verse that she began to see her own sins. "But behold, the Jews were a stiffnecked people; and they despised the words of plainness, and killed the prophets, and sought for things that they could not understand. Wherefore, because of their blindness, which blindness came by *looking beyond the mark,* they must needs fall; for God hath taken away his plainness from them, and delivered unto them many things which they cannot understand, because they desired it. And because they desired it God hath done it, that they may stumble." (Jacob 4:14; emphasis added.)

She came to understand that going beyond the mark can be just as sinful as falling short. To this good woman's credit, she was teachable and began to seek the Lord's direction in solving her marital and family problems. As she became more and more sensitive to following her conscience, which included seeking her husband's forgiveness of her overzealousness (see Mosiah 7:21), she was able to invite a miraculous change in her family. She began to live the principle taught by the Apostle Peter in the New Testament. "Likewise, ye wives, be in subjection to your own husbands; that, if any [husbands] obey not the word, they also may without the word be won by the conduct of the wives; while they behold your chaste conduct coupled with fear" (JST, 1 Peter 3:1–2).

While at first her husband thought her attempts to change were simply attempts at manipulation, he soon became convinced she was sincere and began to do some serious repenting of his own. Please don't misunderstand, at no time did this valiant woman compromise what she felt was the right thing to do, but she came to understand, in the words of Elder Boyd K. Packer, "A virtue when pressed to the extreme may turn into a vice."[7]

Evil for Evil

We are social beings. Our lives have always been and always will be lived in relationships with others. In the Doctrine and Covenants we read that the "same sociality which exists among us here will exist among us there [celestial sphere]" (D&C 130:2). It is in our relationships with others that we have the greatest potential for beauty or pain. Elder Packer has also written that, "No experience can be more beautiful, no power more compelling, more exquisite. Or, if misused, no suffering is more excruciating than that connected with love."[8] While Elder Packer was referring to romantic relationships, I believe that all relationships have potential for great joy or misery. Just as love requires some kind of relationship, so does misery. Note the following example of David and Diane:

> David and Diane had been married for two years. Their relationship had regressed, and criticism filled their conversations together. Neither seemed to be able to find pleasure or happiness in their marriage. They felt their burdens were increased because they were both working long hours and trying to complete their schooling. Their expectations about their marriage were not even remotely being fulfilled. David felt Diane was not spiritual enough and was failing in her duty to support his priesthood decisions. Diane felt her contribution to the family equaled his and that he was constantly judging her unfairly. After a hurtful night of arguing, Diane moved back to her parents' home, convinced that she had made a terrible choice of a husband, an irreversible mistake.
>
> For three weeks they did not see or hear from each other. At first David thought Diane would come back, but she had become reimmersed in the love of her former home and was enjoying the familiarity and security. Meanwhile, David kept reliving in his mind all the wrong things that Diane had done

and how justified his actions were. Each night he prayed to the Lord to help Diane to change, to become a better person, more like the person he thought he had married.

One night, while writing in his journal, he reviewed some of the entries of the preceding months. He became acutely aware of how much criticism of Diane filled those pages. He suddenly realized that his belittling, criticism, and lack of concern for her welfare was a direct contradiction to the spirituality he professed. No wonder she could not support his so-called priesthood decisions. He knelt in prayer, this time with a broken heart and a contrite spirit, and prayed for forgiveness. He prayed, not that the Lord would change Diane, but that the Lord would change him and help him to become the husband Diane thought she had married. This contrition, when humbly offered to Diane, rekindled her willingness to try again. His sincere efforts softened her heart and brought about a new admiration and regard for him.[9]

In the book of Romans the Apostle Paul counseled that we should "recompense to no man evil for evil. Provide things honest in the sight of all men." (Romans 12:17.) However, when others provoke us, the "natural" thing to do is to live the lesser law and exchange "life for life, eye for eye, tooth for tooth, hand for hand, foot for foot, burning for burning, wound for wound, stripe for stripe" (Exodus 21:23–25), or in other words, evil for evil.

As sad as it may seem, sometimes we even rejoice in another's iniquities, because we often use the sins and faults of others as justification for our own. The fact that the other person is treating us badly allows us to maintain our accusatory attitudes towards them and not love them as we should.

When I work with feuding couples, I often hear this phrase, "see . . . see . . . you're doing it again!!" In other words, "Aha, you've just given me the evidence I need for the accusing attitudes I have toward you." Personally, I have never worked with a couple where both parties weren't responsible, at least to some degree, for the problems they were facing.

Even though one of the partners may indeed be less guilty than the other, their own sins, mistakes, or weaknesses will be used by their spouse to justify their unrighteous behavior. This may be to what the scriptures are referring when they speak of the importance of being blameless. Alma wrote: "Have ye walked, keeping yourselves blameless before God? Could ye say, if ye were called to die at this time, within yourselves, that ye have been sufficiently humble?" (Alma 5:27.)

I have come to believe that many of the emotional problems we experience, such as anger, low self-esteem, depression, boredom, anxiety, etc., are actually assertions or judgments we make against others and even ourselves.[10] Contrary to popular opinion, we are not caused to think, feel, or act in the ways we do by the actions of others, they are actions that we initiate.* While many people are threatened by the idea that emotions are judgments, it is actually a very hopeful, liberating truth. If indeed our fallen natures are brought about by our own personal sins, there is a way to be free—repentance and redemption through the Holy Messiah. As Lehi taught: "And the Messiah cometh in the fulness of time, that he may redeem the children of men from the fall. And because they are redeemed from the fall, they have become free forever, knowing good from evil; to act for themselves and not to be acted upon." (2 Nephi 2:26.) On the contrary, if our problems are the effect of a prior cause initiated by someone or something else, there is nothing we can really do about it but wait for our circumstances to change. What a hopeless perspective!

While the fall of Adam and Eve may appear to be a curse, it was in reality a great blessing. The Fall provided Adam and Eve and all mankind the opposition necessary to grow and progress. Note the following words of Adam: "And in that day Adam blessed God and was filled, and began to prophesy concerning

---

* It is possible that we can be involved in behaving negatively for so long that these attitudes can become a part of our natures and be experienced as automatic responses.

all the families of the earth, saying: Blessed be the name of God, for *because of my transgression* my eyes are opened, and in this life I shall have joy, and again in the flesh I shall see God" (Moses 5:10; emphasis added).

As each of us struggle with the problems of life, it is important to remember that there is a great purpose in opposition and adversity. From the writings of President Ezra Taft Benson we read: "It is in the depths where men and women learn the lessons which help them gain strength—not at the pinnacle of success. The hour of man's success is his greatest danger. It sometimes takes reverses to make us appreciate our blessings and to develop into strong, courageous characters. We can meet every reverse that can possibly come with the help of the Lord."[11]

It is important to carefully consider and identify what portion of the various challenges we face comes as a result of our own sins and weaknesses, and then we must do what we can to change, repent, and access the power of the atonement of Christ. King Benjamin taught: "And finally, I cannot tell you all the things whereby ye may commit sin; for there are divers ways and means, even so many that I cannot number them. But this much I can tell you, that if ye do not watch yourselves, and your thoughts, and your words, and your deeds, and observe the commandments of God, and continue in the faith of what ye have heard concerning the coming of our Lord, even unto the end of your lives, ye must perish. And now, O man, remember, and perish not." (Mosiah 4:29–30.)

While much of the grief and trouble we experience in life comes from our own sins and the sins of others, there is also another source. Elder Neal A. Maxwell has written:

> Some things happen to us because of our own mistakes and our own sins. . . .
>
> Still other trials and tribulations come to us merely as a part of living, for, as indicated in the scriptures, the Lord "sendeth rain on the just and on the unjust." (Matthew 5:45.) We are not immunized against all inconvenience and difficulties nor against aging. . . .

There is another dimension of suffering, and other challenges that come to us even though we seem to be innocent. These come to us because an omniscient Lord deliberately chooses to school us: "For whom the Lord loveth he chasteneth, and scourgeth every son whom he receiveth" (Hebrews 12:6); "Nevertheless the Lord seeth fit to chasten his people; yea, he trieth their patience and their faith" (Mosiah 23:21).[12]

The scriptures plainly teach that the Lord gives us weakness that we may be humble, and if we will seek his counsel and have faith in him, our weakness will become strong (see Ether 12:27). Sins can also be overcome, but only through the power of the atonement of Christ. There is no theory, philosophy, or psychotherapy, no matter how elegant, rational, or effective that can cleanse us of sin, except the merits and methods of the restored gospel of Jesus Christ.

NOTES

1. Spencer W. Kimball, *The Teachings of Spencer W. Kimball,* ed. Edward L. Kimball (Salt Lake City: Bookcraft, 1982), p. 155.

2. C. S. Lewis, *The Screwtape Letters* (New York: Macmillan Publishing Company, 1962), p. 56.

3. J. Richard Clarke, "To Honor the Priesthood," *Ensign,* May 1991, p. 42.

4. Professor C. Terry Warner's academic treatment of the subject of anger can be found in his "Anger and Similar Delusions," *The Social Construction of Emotion,* ed. Rom Harre (Oxford: Basil Blackwell, 1986), pp. 135–66.

5. See John W. Welch, *The Sermon at the Temple and the Sermon on the Mount* (Salt Lake City: Deseret Book Co., 1990), p. 162.

6. C. Terry Warner, *Bonds of Anguish, Bonds of Love,* 4:8.

7. Boyd K. Packer, "Covenants," *Ensign,* November 1990, p. 85.

8. Boyd K. Packer, *Eternal Love* (Salt Lake City: Deseret Book Co., 1973), p. 7.

9. In *Teach Them Correct Principles: A Study in Family Relations* (Salt Lake City: The Church of Jesus Christ of Latter-day Saints, 1987), pp. 101–02.

10. See C. Terry Warner, "Anger and Similar Delusions," pp. 135–66.

11. Ezra Taft Benson, *The Teachings of Ezra Taft Benson* (Salt Lake City: Bookcraft, 1988), p. 465.

12. Neal A. Maxwell, *All These Things Shall Give Thee Experience* (Salt Lake City: Deseret Book Co., 1979), pp. 29–30.

7

And God having redeemed man from the fall, men became again, in their infant state, innocent before God.
—D&C 93:38

THE NATURE OF MAN

Our personal views concerning the nature of man can have profound implications for how we live our lives. For example, a parent's beliefs about the nature of children can have important meaning for how they rear them. In Victorian England many parents considered their children to have evil natures because they were "born in sin" as a consequence of Adam and Eve partaking of the fruit of the tree of knowledge of good and evil in the Garden of Eden. Because of this erroneous belief, proposed by protestant theologians such as John Calvin, many parents believed their duties included providing stern discipline even to the extreme of "beating the devil" out of their children.[1] Some historians believe that the phrase *rule of thumb* originated in England as parents were instructed that they could not discipline their children with a rod (stick) any larger in diameter than their thumb.[2] The idea that a child is born evil, which is still believed by some, can lead to harsh, rigid parenting and even outright physical violence in some cases. Examples of this can be found in the writings of some traditional Christian psychologists. While I applaud much of the work done by these men and women some of their counsel regarding the rearing of children tends to be a little heavy-handed. It is hard to fault them for this, because their work is simply a reflection of protestant theology. What a privilege it is for us to have the clarification provided by the Book of Mormon and other scriptures of the Restoration!

Children as Noble Savages

Another tradition we find in our midst was first proposed by the French philosopher Jean-Jacques Rousseau (1712–1778). Rousseau considered children to be born good and simply in need of a warm, supportive, nurturing environment to grow into healthy adults. Parents and the culture of which they were a part were seen by Rousseau as being the cause of most of the problems experienced by children and later by adults. Rousseau believed that if parents would allow their children to express themselves in their own unique ways and leave them more to themselves, they would be much more likely to achieve their greatest potentials.[3] Rousseau once wrote, "Man is born free, and everywhere he is in chains."[4] In other words, Rousseau believed children are naturally good, but become enslaved by a corrupt culture. This philosophy is the foundation for many of the popular psychology theories of parenting today.

If the limitations of Rousseau's humanistic philosophy are not understood properly, believing and practicing these ideas can contribute to serious problems for the family and for all of humanity. If the parents believe that a child is naturally good, they may be more inclined to *indulge* their children by allowing them to have total freedom of choice in what they choose to do. Indulgence, called *free agency* by the indulgent, is the adversary's counterfeit of what the Lord has termed *moral agency*. Elder Boyd K. Packer exemplifies this point of doctrine in his discussion of "pro-choice" philosophy:

> Regardless of how lofty and moral the "pro-choice" argument sounds, it is badly flawed. With that same logic one could argue that all traffic signs and barriers which keep the careless from danger should be pulled down on the theory

that each individual must be free to choose how close to the edge he will go.

The phrase *"free agency"* does not appear in scripture. The only agency spoken of there is *moral agency,* "which," the Lord said, "I have given unto him, that every man may be *accountable* for his own sins in the day of judgment." (D&C 101:78; italics added.)[5]

Another contention raised is that we are free to choose what we do with our bodies. To a certain extent this is true for all of us. We are free to think, feel, plan, and do, but once an action has been taken, we are never free from its consequences. For example, a couple may choose to have an abortion, but there are both mortal and eternal consequences for them and for the baby they are aborting. Reaping what we sow is an eternal principle. It is important that we understand and teach that the agency spoken of in scripture doesn't simply imply the choice between alternatives, but the choice between right and wrong.

Children as Blank Slates

The English philosopher John Locke (1632–1704) raised concerns about the contradictory philosophies of Calvin and Rousseau and proposed that children are born neither good nor evil, but as *tabula rasa* or "blank slates." Locke proposed that children develop and their personalities form as they are acted upon by the environment. American psychologist John Watson, whose teachings follow the Lockean tradition, once wrote: "Give me a dozen healthy infants, well-formed, and my own specified world to bring them up in and I'll guarantee to take any one at random and train him to become any specialist I might select—doctor, lawyer, artist, merchant, chief, and yes, even beggarman and thief, regardless of his talents, penchants, tendencies, abilities, vocations, and race of his ancestors."[6]

These words reinforce the idea that children are products of

their environments. Locke's and Watson's ideas are the prede-
cessors of the more scientific theories of child development in
use today. One of the greatest weaknesses in this theory is
found in its implications for parenting. Many parents who believe their child is born as a "blank slate" typically feel a great
responsibility to make something of the child. These parents
characteristically believe that if their child is going to amount
to anything in life, it is going to be the result of their successful
parenting. Conversely, the other side of this counterfeit philosophy could lead parents to believe that if their child has problems or challenges, or isn't a "success," it is also the fault of the
parent. Parents who have these kinds of beliefs will often attempt to have their child enrolled in multiple extracurricular
activities. It is not uncommon for a child to be enrolled in
piano lessons, singing lessons, gymnastics, computer class, soc-
cer, T-ball, and karate all at the same time! This philosophy is
represented by the statement, "if it is to be (my child amount-
ing to something), it is up to me!" One writer described the
child who participates in such a lifestyle as "The Hurried
Child."[7] Sadly enough, another implication of this style of parenting is the mother feeling that it is necessary to work outside
the home in order to afford the fee for these extra activities.

The kinds of false beliefs I have presented so far are a portion of what the scriptures refer to as "the wicked and abominable traditions of their fathers" (Helaman 15:7). It is imperative we come to understand these false doctrines for what they
are and then recognize the truths of which they are a counterfeit: "And behold, ye do know of yourselves, for ye have witnessed it, that as many of them as are brought to the knowledge of the truth, and to know of the wicked and abominable
traditions of their fathers, and are led to believe the holy scriptures, yea, the prophecies of the holy prophets, which are written, which leadeth them to faith on the Lord, and unto repentance, which faith and repentance bringeth a change of heart
unto them—" (Helaman 15:7).

When I ask my students to choose between these three al-
ternative views of the nature of children (Calvin, Rousseau, and

Locke), the vote is usually split between Calvin and Rousseau. Those espousing Calvin's view will quote King Benjamin's discourse wherein he writes, "The natural man is an enemy to God, and has been from the fall of Adam" (Mosiah 3:19). Those favoring Rousseau's view of the innate goodness of children will typically quote the words of Christ in Mormon's letter to his son Moroni: "Wherefore, little children are whole, for they are not capable of committing sin; wherefore the curse of Adam is taken from them in me, that it hath no power over them. . . . Little children need no repentance, neither baptism." (Moroni 8:8, 11.)

Which one of these views is right? My vote is none of the above. The scriptures, while supporting parts of these various theories, teach something quite different. From the Doctrine and Covenants we can read the words of the Lord on the subject: "Every spirit of man was *innocent* in the beginning; and God having redeemed man from the fall, men became again, in their infant state, *innocent* before God" (D&C 93:38; emphasis added). Being born innocent means that at birth we are neither good nor evil, but have potential for both. Some may argue that being born innocent is the same as being born as a "blank slate." The difference between these two assertions is found in the fact that as children mature they are free "to act for themselves and not to be acted upon" (2 Nephi 2:26; see also Helaman 14:30). The "blank slate" idea espouses the notion that as a child matures he continues to be a passive object conditioned by the environment. The scriptures teach that as innocent children mature they become active agents, free to choose good or evil. In the Book of Mormon we read: "Wherefore, men are free according to the flesh; and all things are given them which are expedient unto man. And they are *free to choose* liberty and eternal life, through the great Mediator of all men, or to choose captivity and death, according to the captivity and power of the devil; for he seeketh that all men might be miserable like unto himself." (2 Nephi 2:27; emphasis added. See also 2 Nephi 10:23; Alma 13:3; Helaman 14:31.)

While we have the potential to become like God we also

have the potential to become like the devil. The choice is ours, not in some preformed, predestined fate. We must come to understand the mission the Lord has for each of us. It is only in fulfilling the measures and purposes of our creations that we will experience the meaning and joy each of us seek.

The Fall

The Lord continues, in section ninety-three of the Doctrine and Covenants, his description of how each of us lose our innocence and become the "natural man." "And that wicked one cometh and taketh away light and truth, through disobedience, from the children of men, and because of the tradition of their fathers" (D&C 93:39). As we disobey the commandments of God and suffer the consequences of believing and living the incorrect traditions of our fathers, we become fallen. In the Doctrine and Covenants we read: "And that he created man, male and female, after his own image and in his own likeness, created he them; and gave unto them commandments that they should love and serve him, the only living and true God, and that he should be the only being whom they should worship. But by the transgression of these holy laws man became sensual and devilish, and became fallen man." (D&C 20:18–20; see also Moses 5:13.)

Our fallen natures also come as a result of sins that are not our own. As I alluded to in the previous chapter, if a child grows up in a home where alcohol is used freely, the chances are good that he will not see it as a sin. This child, however, will still suffer the consequences if he consumes alcohol. He is also developing traditions and appetites that will be carried forward into his later life. The same is true of other incorrect traditions—we suffer the consequences of sinning, even if we are sinning in ignorance (see Mosiah 3:11).

In my work with families over the years I have come to believe that one of the most important things parents can do for their children (and for themselves) is to identify and become free of the incorrect traditions that are so much a part of our society. One example of this is the way in which anger and contention are becoming an accepted way of life. Elder Russell M. Nelson has stated:

> My concern is that contention is becoming accepted as a way of life. From what we see and hear in the media, the classroom, and the workplace, all are now infected to some degree with contention. How easy it is, yet how wrong it is, to allow habits of contention to pervade matters of spiritual significance, because contention is forbidden by divine decree:
> "The Lord God hath commanded that men should not murder; that they should not lie; that they should not steal; that they should not take the name of the Lord their God in vain; that they should not envy; that they should not have malice; that they should not contend one with another." (2 Nephi 26:32.)[8]

How many television shows can you name where contention, sarcasm, and other insults are the basis for the entire program? Many of these shows even have laugh tracks dubbed in to reinforce the producer's and director's desired response.

While the ungodly aspects of our personalities—contention, pride, lust, and greed—are natural and even normal parts of the human experience, are they characteristics we should simply learn to accept? Many of us are familiar with those who say things like, "That's just the way I am," or "I am a Judd, and that's just the way Judds are!" Even popular books that describe various personality traits in terms of planets, colors, birth order, or astrological signs should, in my opinion, be read with caution. These explanations of personality, while interesting and descriptive, can, if we are not very careful, become rationalizations we employ to justify our judgments of others and to avoid the need for change in our own lives.

The real solution to our problems comes not in acceptance and compromise, but in personal change. King Benjamin defined both the problem and the solution in the following: "For the natural man is an enemy to God, and has been from the fall of Adam, and will be, forever and ever, unless he yields to the enticings of the Holy Spirit, and putteth off the natural man and becometh a saint through the atonement of Christ the Lord, and becometh as a child, submissive, meek, humble, patient, full of love, willing to submit to all things which the Lord seeth fit to inflict upon him, even as a child doth submit to his father" (Mosiah 3:19).

Each of us is the "natural man" to a greater or lesser degree. It is only by "yielding to the enticings of the Holy Spirit" that we may begin to make the changes that are needed in our lives. Consider the following story of a good friend of mine:

> I had grown up in the Church, served a successful mission, and believed in the gospel, but somehow I never felt the happiness I had always sought. I married, but soon found my unhappiness to go in cycles as I would make the effort to pray and be obedient, but then would quit seeking divine help. Too many times I tried to rely on my own strength and knowledge to work out life's problems. I found myself during these times becoming intolerant of the mistakes of others and angry when my agenda was not met. At times I would attempt to control my family by ignoring them and withholding affection.
>
> Eventually this pattern of living and contention led to physical confrontations with my wife. Sometimes I would become angry, without warning, to insignificant provocations. I would then feel awful and go through the repentance process and resolve to do better. But why did it not stick? Gradually the same patterns came back.
>
> My wife and I went to many counselors seeking help with our marriage relationship. We were taught to communicate more effectively, we found out why we behaved in certain ways because of our gender, and learned skills to cope with stress and outside influences. "Change your behavior" I was told time after time. But nothing seemed to change; our relationship became worse and ended in divorce. The pain was immense, I didn't understand what to do or how to change.
>
> Lucky for me, a loving bishop took me under his wing. I truly felt his love for me, which softened my heart to his counsel. He pointed me to the Atonement and helped me under-

stand that only Jesus Christ could bring about the change I searched for. I believed his words and began searching and learning about the Atonement. Most of my adult life I had believed in Christ, but I never believed that his promises were for me. As I began understanding what the Atonement was all about, my heart changed. I no longer had desires to chose evil but to do good in my life. I found myself pouring out my soul to my God in prayer many times throughout the day, asking that my faith in Christ would increase and that my heart would be filled with love. I found that the more I sought after him, the more I could feel his love and assurance.

Day by day my faith increases, I have hope in those wonderful promises that I see all through the scriptures. I have found great peace because of the love I feel for my Father in Heaven. The best part of all of this is the desires I have to love those around me. There is peace in my home. My relationship with my children has reached new levels, and I look for opportunities to serve and help others.

Like all of us, this individual was born innocent, but through his own sins and the sins of his fathers (see D&C 93:38–39), he became an angry, and sometimes violent person. What happened next is best described by Alma, for "according to his faith there was a mighty change wrought in his heart" (Alma 5:12). What a strength and comfort it is to know that no matter what our sins and weaknesses are or what kind of a person we have become, "with God nothing can be impossible" (JST, Luke 1:37).

NOTES

1. Philippe Aries, *Centuries of Childhood: A Social History of Family Life,* trans. Robert Baldick (New York: Knopf, 1962), pp. 128–33.

2. Ian Gibson, *The English Vice: Beating, Sex and Shame in Victorian England and After* (London: Duckworth, 1978), p. 49.

3. William C. Crain, *Theories of Development: Concepts and Applications,* 3d ed. (Englewood, N.J.: Prentice Hall, 1992), pp. 8–10.

4. Jean-Jacques Rousseau, *The Social Contract,* trans. G. Hopkins (New York: Oxford University Press, 1962), p. 1.

5. Boyd K. Packer, "Our Moral Environment," *Ensign,* May 1992, pp. 66–67.

6. B. F. Skinner, *Behaviorism* (New York: W. W. Norton & Co., Inc., 1925), p. 104.

7. David Elkind, *The Hurried Child: Growing Up Too Fast Too Soon,* 2d ed. (Reading, Mass.: Addison-Wesley, 1988), p. xi.

8. Russell M. Nelson, "The Canker of Contention," *Ensign,* May 1989, p. 68.

8

SELF-IMAGE AND THE IMAGE OF GOD

We live in a society that has placed mortal man at the center of attention. Self-esteem has replaced sanctification, and loving ourselves has supplanted the love of God and the love of our fellowman. In many ways we have become our own gods as the needs of self have become the focus of our lives. This form of latter-day idolatry is what the Apostle Paul was describing when he wrote, "in the last days perilous times shall come. For men shall be lovers of their own selves." (2 Timothy 3:1–2.) President Ezra Taft Benson warned us that pride is one of Satan's most effective tools and can "cause a man or a woman to center so much attention on self that he or she becomes insensitive to their Creator or fellow beings."[1]

During my graduate training in counseling psychology, I had the opportunity of working with men and women who were struggling with a serious psychological and physical problem called anorexia nervosa. This is a condition where women (and sometimes men) will starve themselves and lose drastic amounts of weight to the extent that their lives are in jeopardy.

As I came to know and understand some of the concerns of the people I was working with, it soon became apparent that their lives were consumed with thoughts and fears concerning food, weight, and physical appearances. In many cases their obsession with body image wasn't so much that they were guilty of vanity, as it was that their weight was one of the few things in their lives they could control; food and flesh had become both enemy and ally. Soon after my training with these individuals began I realized that my strategies to help them gain weight were making me an enemy as well. Some of these young women would do almost anything to make it appear that they were gaining weight so they could be released from the hospital. In truth, many of them continued to lose weight while attempting to outwit the hospital staff into believing otherwise. The ultimate reality of this deception was the fact that if these young women continued to starve themselves they could eventually become so physically compromised they would die. However, simply regaining the weight wasn't the solution either. If they simply regained the weight they had lost, they would be back where they started—miserable. It soon became apparent to me that these young women were ensnared in what the Apostle Paul called a "strait betwixt two" (Philippians 1:23). Today, we would call this a dilemma or describe it as "being caught between a rock and a hard place." I have come to believe that what we call dilemmas are often false dichotomies (see Alma 7:18–20). In other words, the only choices we feel we have are really choices between competing falsehoods.

For these young women, gaining weight wasn't the answer, but neither was losing it. As they would lose weight, they would feel a false sense of esteem and control, and as they would gain weight, this sense of esteem and control would turn to despair. The greatest problem, from their perspective, was that the weight they lost was never enough. In reality, their goal of having the perfect body, or having ultimate control, was an illusive fantasy which was impossible to fulfill. Samuel the Lamanite used the word *slippery* (see Helaman 13:31) in connection with the Nephite's attempts at reaching for the wrong goals. The Nephites believed that peace was to be found in riches; the young women I have been describing had come to believe that happiness was always five to ten pounds away or in having their hip bones show through their clothing. Their lives became a never-ending cycling between the "high self-esteem" generated from weight loss and the "low self-esteem" which came from weight gain.

One afternoon as I conducted a workshop for those with eating disorders, I was impressed with a few similarities between their stories and some of the struggles that I had experienced as a young athlete. As a ballplayer it seemed that even though I was privileged to have experienced a great deal of success, no matter how successful I was, it was never enough. I could never score enough touchdowns, make as many points, or strike out a sufficient number of batters to feel that my performance was acceptable. I too nearly died in my attempts to control the perceptions of others. While I wasn't starving myself, I was breaking bones, tearing cartilage, experiencing concussions, being stitched, dislocating joints, and undergoing surgery, all the while trying to prove to myself and others that I was of worth. I have come to believe that our culture's obsession with success, self-esteem, self-actualization, and self-image are contributing factors to many of the problems we face today.

Other self-centered obsessions include measuring our self-worth by such artificial standards as wealth and position. So many of us are obsessed with the make and model of the cars we drive, the labels on our clothes, our academic degrees, our occupations, our income, our Church callings, the neighborhoods we live in, how many children we have, and a host of other labels designed to prove our worth. The problem is that happiness and prosperity, measured by such standards, are deceptions. Note the counsel given by the Lord to one of the early members of the Church concerning his desire to excel: "And also let my servant William W. Phelps stand in the office to which I have appointed him, and receive his inheritance in the land; and also he hath need to repent, for I, the Lord, am not well pleased with him, for he seeketh to excel, and he is not sufficiently meek before me" (D&C 58:40–41).

I do not know exactly what it was that Brother Phelps was trying to do that prompted the Lord to call him to repentance, but we do know that William Wines Phelps was an accomplished writer, editor, and musician. Perhaps he too was consumed with pleasing himself and others and not the Lord. In the following statement President Ezra Taft Benson succinctly identifies both the problem and the solution to the challenges I have been describing: "The proud depend upon the world to tell them whether they have value or not. Their self-esteem is determined by where they are judged to be on the ladders of worldly success. They feel worthwhile as individuals if the numbers beneath them in achievement, talent, beauty, or intellect are large enough. Pride is ugly. It says, 'If you succeed, I am a failure.' If we love God, do His will, and fear His judgment more than men's, we will have self-esteem."[2]

I have a good friend who graduated from medical school and became a physician in his late twenties. After practicing medicine for a few years he decided that being a doctor wasn't for him. He then went to law school, after which he earned his MBA (master of business administration). At the present time he is considering yet another career move and is in the process of divorcing his second wife and marrying one of his business associates. My heart aches for him, he has no sense of who he is or what his mission in life is all about. In my opinion, his sense of self is fragile and slippery because it is not founded on his relationship with God.

Someone has said, "you can't be too thin or too rich." Whoever said this has never known someone living with anorexia, or someone obsessed with being the best, or someone determined to "get ahead" financially. Being thin or rich gives some people a feeling of esteem and power, but it is a deception. C. S. Lewis has said, "Pride gets no pleasure out of having something, only out of having more of it than the next man."[3] Living in this manner makes our happiness always dependent upon our relative position to others. Meeting someone whom we judge as wealthier, more attractive or whose occupation we consider to be more prestigious than ours, tends to depress us, while meeting someone whom we consider beneath us feeds our ego.

In reality, most of us have some things in common with the individuals I have been describing, whether our obsessions be with physical appearance, money, education, position—all are designed to enhance our self-image by appealing to the approval of others. The Apostle Paul described those of us who deal with such problems as "menpleasers" (Ephesians 6:6). I have found that to experience any lasting and meaningful changes in regard to these kinds of problems we must come to see things as they really are. The prophet Jacob counseled: "Behold, my brethren, he that prophesieth, let him prophesy to the understanding of men; for the Spirit speaketh the truth and lieth not. Wherefore, it speaketh of things as they really are, and of things as they really will be; wherefore, these things are manifested unto us plainly, for the salvation of our souls." (Jacob 4:13.)

On an intellectual level, the women I have described earlier could understand that their eating disorder was destroying their lives, but they couldn't see a way out. What should they do—gain thirty pounds and learn to live with it? Should those who are wealthy sell all they have and give the proceeds to charity? Individuals with whom I have been blessed to have worked, who have overcome problems involving such obsessions, have come to an understanding that there is a difference between what many call high self-esteem and what the scriptures describe as confidence. The following dialogue between Ammon and Aaron illustrates this difference. Ammon begins the dialogue and Aaron quickly responds:

> Blessed be the name of our God; let us sing to his praise, yea, let us give thanks to his holy name, for he doth work righteousness forever.
>
> For if we had not come up out of the land of Zarahemla, these our dearly beloved brethren, who have so dearly beloved us, would still have been racked with hatred against us, yea, and they would also have been strangers to God.

And it came to pass that when Ammon had said these words, his brother Aaron rebuked him, saying: Ammon, I fear that thy joy doth carry thee away unto boasting.

But Ammon said unto him: I do not boast in my own strength, nor in my own wisdom; but behold, my joy is full, yea, my heart is brim with joy, and I will rejoice in my God.

Yea, I know that I am nothing; as to my strength I am weak; therefore I will not boast of myself, but I will boast of my God, for in his strength I can do all things; yea, behold, many mighty miracles we have wrought in this land, for which we will praise his name forever. (Alma 26:8–12.)

Ammon's success, confidence, and subsequent joy, did not come because of his faith in himself, but from his faith in God. Ammon had learned that he, in and of himself, was nothing, but with God he could "do all things" (Alma 26:12). Ammon's expression of his own nothingness is similar to that of the prophet Moses after he had encountered the Lord on Mount Sinai: "And it came to pass that it was for the space of many hours before Moses did again receive his natural strength like unto man; and he said unto himself: Now, for this cause I know that man is nothing, which thing I never had supposed" (Moses 1:10).

Moses' description of his nothingness shouldn't be confused with low self-esteem which, in the words of Ezra Taft Benson, can actually be a more common form of pride. "Most of us consider pride to be a sin of those on the top, such as the rich and the learned, looking down at the rest of us. (See 2 Nephi 9:42.) There is, however, a far more common ailment among us—and that is pride from the bottom looking up. It is manifest in so many ways, such as faultfinding, gossiping, backbiting, murmuring, living beyond our means, envying, coveting, withholding gratitude and praise that might lift another, and being unforgiving and jealous."[4]

A focus on self is most often a selfish preoccupation with our own needs and wants, while confidence and meekness come by seeking to follow the will of our Heavenly Father to bless the lives of others. In the words of the Savior, "whosoever will save his life shall lose it: and whosoever will lose his life for my sake shall find it" (Matthew 16:25). As mentioned earlier, President Benson stated, "If we love God, do His will, and fear His judgment more than men's, we will have self-esteem."[5] Sister Patricia Holland described the importance of our faith in God this way:

> I will never forget the first time Jeff tried to kiss me. We were standing in the entryway of my home when my mother unexpectedly walked into the room and caught him in the act. Jeff, being the fast thinker he is, said, "Hi, Sister Terry. Pat and I were just trading gum."
>
> Later my mother, in retelling the incident to my father, said, "Jeff's confidence in a difficult situation amazes me. The fact that he can think that fast on his feet will certainly ensure his success."
>
> My father smiled at me and said, "Confidence is a great blessing to anyone who has it. But Jeff is also smart enough to know what to have confidence in. Both of you need to re-member that your greatest strength and surest success will come through humility and dependence upon the Lord."[6]

The kind of confidence or self-esteem the Lord would have us experience can only be found in letting go of our own self-centered desires and fulfilling the Lord's will for us by exercising faith in him. The Lord counseled the prophet Joseph, "let virtue garnish thy thoughts unceasingly; then shall thy confidence wax strong in the presence of God" (D&C 121:45).

NOTES

1. Ezra Taft Benson, "This Is a Day of Sacrifice," *Ensign*, May 1979, p. 34.

2. Ezra Taft Benson, "Beware of Pride," *Ensign*, May 1989, p. 6.

3. C. S. Lewis, *Mere Christianity* (New York: Macmillan Publishing Company, 1960), p. 109.

4. Ezra Taft Benson, "Beware of Pride," p. 5.

5. Ibid., p. 6.

6. Patricia Holland, "Becoming 'Meek and Lowly in Heart'," *Brigham Young University 1985–86 Devotional and Fireside Speeches* (Provo: University Publications, 1986), p. 57.

SECTION THREE

The Atonement

9

According to the great plan of the Eternal God
there must be an atonement made, or else
all mankind must unavoidably perish.
—Alma 34:9

THERE MUST BE AN
ATONEMENT MADE

While there is much we can do as individuals, families, and communities to experience peace in this life and eternal life in the world to come, each of us, in one sense or another, remains in a fallen state and is under the bondages of sin, tradition, and mortality. In the Book of Mormon we read, "all are hardened; yea, all are fallen and are lost, and must perish except it be through the atonement" (Alma 34:9). There has been only one who lived a life without sin, and even the Savior suffered the sins of others as well as his own physical pain and eventual death.

Contrary to the beliefs of some, the perfect person doesn't exist (with the exception of heavenly beings). I've never witnessed a perfect marriage or a family without flaw. The scriptures plainly teach that everyone (who has reached the age of accountability) is guilty of sin, and that we all have weakness (see Romans 3:23; Ether 12:27). No matter what our personal possessions are—power, prominence, prestige, intellect, health, wealth, or even righteousness, we cannot save ourselves from our own sins nor can we perfect our own weaknesses. Each one of us is in vital need of the atonement of Jesus Christ. The prophet Lehi taught: "Wherefore, how great the importance to make these things known unto the inhabitants of the earth, that they may know that there is no flesh that can dwell in the presence of God, save it be through the merits, and mercy, and grace of the Holy Messiah" (2 Nephi 2:8).

King Benjamin instructed his people, "There shall be no other name given nor any other way nor means whereby salvation can come unto the children of men, only in and through the name of Christ, the Lord Omnipotent" (Mosiah 3:17). Therapists, medications, physicians, talk-show hosts, politicians, athletes, philosophers, seminars, and best-sellers come and go, but they all have something in common—none of them can save us nor can they give us the everlasting joy and peace each of us seeks. The Apostle Peter proclaimed, "there is none other name under heaven given among men, whereby we must be saved" (Acts 4:12). The Savior taught, "I am the way, the truth, and the life: no man cometh unto the Father, but by me" (John 14:6). There is no other way to fulfill our mission in this life and gain eternal life in the world to come than by following Jesus Christ.

As a young missionary I once felt threatened by those of other faiths who continually wanted to discuss the grace of Christ. Invariably, these individuals would want to discuss the Apostle Paul's teachings concerning grace found in Ephesians 2:8–9; while my companions and I would counter their arguments by stressing the importance of works (see James 2:14–20).[1] We even had a name for our born-again Christian foes—*gracers.* Though some of these people had a distorted view of the doctrine of grace and believed that salvation would be theirs even if they were living sinful lives, I have since come to understand that there were others who had a much better understanding of grace and the atonement of Christ than did I. I am ashamed to admit it, but for the most part, I treated these *gracers* with contempt. I am saddened when I contemplate the possibility that my ill will may have prevented some from investigating the Church further. I now realize that through my arrogant ignorance, not only was I less of the ambassador of

Christ I was called to be, but I had also failed to realize the full power of grace in my own life. Oh, how I wish I had understood the doctrine of the Atonement better than I did! Not just for my sake, but especially for the people I was sent to teach.

The adversary will do all in his power to confuse us; he is a master of counterfeit and has a host of distorted doctrines designed to disable and destroy. Living a righteous life is obviously important, but our own good works will not save us. The Book of Mormon prophet Jacob taught what would become of us had there been no atonement: "Wherefore, it must needs be an infinite atonement—save it should be an infinite atonement this corruption could not put on incorruption [resurrection]. . . . And our spirits must have become like unto . . . devils, angels to a devil, to be shut out from the presence of our God, and to remain with the father of lies, in misery." (2 Nephi 9:7, 9.) Even with good works, without the Atonement, each of us would become like unto the devil himself—not a good identity to retain for eternity.

In addition to the eternal consequences of the Atonement, this central event in the history of the world has profound meaning for mortality as well. For those of us who are struggling with problems—failing marital or family relationships, depression, anxiety, economic problems, health concerns, doubts, or loneliness—a life sincerely centered on Christ is the only complete answer. Most of us have had the experience of working on a problem for which we just can't seem to find the answer. The phrase, "whatever the mind can conceive and believe it can achieve" just doesn't seem to hold true. Many of us have tried one proposed solution after another only to find that none of them work. The following statement from the British philosopher C. S. Lewis teaches us of our own impotence and the centrality of the atonement of Jesus Christ in the process of change:

> When I come to my evening prayers and try to reckon up the sins of the day, nine times out of ten the most obvious one is some sin against charity; I have sulked or snapped or sneered or snubbed or stormed. And the excuse that immediately springs

to my mind is that the provocation was so sudden and un-expected: I was caught off my guard, I had not time to collect myself. . . . Surely what a man does when he is taken off his guard is the best evidence for what sort of man he is? Surely what pops out before the man has time to put on a disguise is the truth? If there are rats in a cellar you are most likely to see them if you go in very suddenly. But the suddenness does not create the rats: it only prevents them from hiding. In the same way the suddenness of the provocation does not make me an ill-tempered man: it only shows me what an ill-tempered man I am. . . . Now that cellar is out of reach of my conscious will. I can to some extent control my acts: I have no direct control over my temperament. And if (as I said before) what we are matters even more than what we do—if indeed, what we do matters chiefly as evidence of what we are—then it follows that the change which I most need to undergo is a change that my own direct, voluntary efforts cannot bring about. And this applies to my good actions too. How many of them were done for the right motive? . . . But I cannot, by direct moral effort, give myself new motives. After the first few steps in the Christian life we realise that everything which really needs to be done in our souls can be done only by God.[2]

Lewis's words remind us that the key to our salvation and exaltation has more to do with the righteousness of the Re-deemer than with our own mortal efforts (see 2 Nephi 2:3). We cannot save ourselves no matter how many casseroles we bake, home teaching visits we make, or temple excursions we take. This is what Paul was addressing when he wrote, "For by grace are ye saved through faith; and that *not of yourselves:* it is the gift of God: not of works, lest any man should boast" (Ephesians 2:8–9; emphasis added).

But in our acceptance of the grace of Christ, we must al-ways remember that "it is by grace that we are saved, *after all we can do*" (2 Nephi 25:23; emphasis added). Just as the adver-sary has seduced some into believing they can work their way to heaven, others have accepted the notion of "cheap grace" and believe that as long as they have accepted Christ, faithfulness doesn't matter (see James 2:24). The Apostle Paul, knowing that some would interpret his emphasis on grace as an excuse for sin, wrote: "What then? shall we sin, because we are not under the law, but under grace? God forbid" (Romans 6:15); Paul obviously understood the importance of living a righteous life. Paul wrote much about grace and less about works because he was attempting to help the people realize that the law of Moses, which the Israelites had practiced for two thousand years, would not save them.

The Joseph Smith Translation of Paul's words to the Romans offers important insight into the proper relationship of grace and works: "Therefore ye are justified of faith and works, through grace" (JST, Romans 4:16). In other words, if we truly have faith in Christ we will receive his grace and keep his commandments. Those who accept Christ and then refuse to keep the commandments are not being honest and true to the covenants they have made. The Apostle John taught, "He that saith, I know him [Jesus Christ], and keepeth not his commandments, is a liar, and the truth is not in him" (1 John 2:4). We must also be sincere in our recognition of our own sins and the need we have for the Savior. The Prophet Lehi taught: "Behold, he [Christ] offereth himself a sacrifice for sin, to answer the ends of the law, unto all those who have a broken heart and a contrite spirit; and unto none else can the ends of the law be answered" (2 Nephi 2:7).

The full intensiveness, beauty, and power of the atonement of Jesus Christ can be experienced only by those who have a broken heart and a contrite spirit. President Benson counseled us that "repentance involves not just a change of actions, but a change of heart."[3] Note the following experience of one of my former students as she began to understand this important truth:

When I first stopped to think about what a broken heart and a contrite spirit are, I was confused. A "broken heart" seemed to be connected with the suffering a girl would experience after being dumped by her boyfriend, and I couldn't understand why we should feel that way or even *want* to feel that way. Why would Heavenly Father and Jesus Christ want us to be devastated all the time? A "contrite spirit" had no meaning to me whatsoever. I was not even sure what the word *contrite* meant. Because of my misunderstanding, I tended to skip over this part of Christ's gospel and hope it really wasn't what it sounded like.

When I came to BYU as a freshman I began to encounter feelings of depression I had first experienced in high school. One thing after another occurred until I could stand it no longer. One night I was on the brink of falling apart and went to my bed and began to cry uncontrollably. I was acting irrationally, and my roommates could tell this was no ordinary release of emotion. They immediately called my mom and told her what was happening. She tried to console me over the telephone, but nothing seemed to work. I went back to bed and crawled into my cave of sorrow. Why was this happening to me? I thought of the pain I was suffering. It seemed so horrible; I couldn't even imagine what Christ must have experienced when he suffered for all the depression of humanity— let alone all their sins, sicknesses, and other pains.

In the dark shroud of my depression it is often hard for the Spirit of the Lord to reach me. However, when I began to calm down I received the answer to my question—*Heavenly Father was allowing me to be broken.* He wanted me to grow, and this was one way to do it. When I emerged from my depression, I would have the qualities of a broken heart and a contrite spirit. I would want to change, be humble, and most important, I would understand that the best way to handle my trials was to submit my will to the Lord's. He knew what he was doing, and I should be grateful that he was taking the time to help me grow. That night, I gained some insight into what a broken heart and a contrite spirit are.[4]

It is important to realize, as did this young woman, that our feelings of despair can be our schoolmasters and serve as invitations for us to come unto Christ: "Come unto me, all ye that labour and are heavy laden, and I will give you rest. Take my yoke upon you, and learn of me; for I am meek and lowly in heart: and ye shall find rest unto your souls. For my yoke is easy, and my burden is light." (Matthew 11:28–30.) The yoke of which the Savior is referring to is a symbolic representation of the relationship he is inviting us to have with him as we strive to keep the covenants we make with our Father in Heaven. One of my colleagues, Stephen Robinson, in his book *Believing Christ,* has described our relationship with the Savior by comparing it with the marital relationship of husband and wife:

> When Janet and I got married, my checking account was over-drawn, but Janet had money in hers. After the wedding, we went to the bank and merged our accounts to create a single, joint account. As far as the bank was concerned, I was no longer just Stephen Robinson, and she was no longer just Janet Bowen. Now we were Stephen and Janet Robinson. A new partnership had been created that included the assets and liabilities of both its component parts. And since Janet had more assets than I had liabilities, the new account had a positive balance. It was like a miracle! Just by entering into a marriage covenant and becoming one with Janet, I was on firm financial ground for the first time in months.[5]

Just as Brother and Sister Robinson entered into a covenant relationship with their Father in Heaven through marriage, each of us has the opportunity of entering into a covenant relationship with God at various times throughout our lives. As we take these covenants seriously, all of our sins (debts) become his and all that he has (assets) becomes ours (see D&C 84:33–40; Romans 8:17).

The covenants with which we are most familiar are those we make at baptism and renew during the sacrament. Most every Sunday we have the opportunity of participating in the covenants associated with the sacrament prayer: "O God, the Eternal Father, we ask thee in the name of thy Son, Jesus Christ, to bless and sanctify this bread to the souls of all those who partake of it; that they may eat in remembrance of the body of thy Son, and witness unto thee, O God, the Eternal Father, that they are willing to take upon them the name of thy Son, and always remember him, and keep his commandments which he hath given them, that they may always have his Spirit to be with them. Amen." (Moroni 4:3.) We covenant with our Heavenly Father that we are willing to take upon ourselves the name of Jesus Christ, always remember him, and keep the commandments. In return we are promised that we will have the Holy Ghost to be our constant companion. The presence of the Holy Ghost in our lives is an important reminder to each of us that we are living "in Christ" (Moroni 10:32) and that our covenant relationship with Heavenly Father is in force.

It has been my experience that most members of the Church do not understand that partaking of the sacrament worthily is, in effect, like being baptized a second time. If we have sincerely repented of our sins and are honestly willing to renew our covenants, we may be forgiven! President Packer has stated: "Generally we understand that, conditioned upon repentance, the ordinance of baptism washes our sins away. Some wonder if they were baptized too soon. If only they could be baptized now and have a clean start. But that is not necessary! Through the ordinance of the sacrament you renew the covenants made at baptism. When you meet all of the conditions of repentance, however difficult, you may be forgiven and your transgressions will trouble your mind no more."[6]

What a joy it is to explain to an individual who, because of transgression, has not been allowed to partake of the sacrament, that the time has come to renew covenants and be completely clean before the Lord, just as if they were rebaptized. What a miracle for each of us! Forgiveness is not even dependent upon our knowing how the process works; the good news is that it does! President Packer further explained: "You need not know everything before the power of the Atonement will work for you. Have faith in Christ; it begins to work the day you ask!"[7]

NOTES

1. President Joseph Fielding Smith stated: "I desire to point out wherein there is no conflict whatever in the teachings of these two apostles of old. . . . Paul was dealing with the class of people who believed that a man could not be saved unless he subscribed to the law of Moses, . . . James on the other hand was defending the necessity of works, counteracting the idea which prevailed among others, who professed faith in Christ, that if they had faith it was all-sufficient." (*Doctrines of Salvation,* comp. Bruce R. McConkie, 3 vols. [Salt Lake City: Bookcraft, 1954–56], 2:307.)

2. C. S. Lewis, *Mere Christianity* (New York: Macmillan Publishing Company, 1960), pp. 164–65.

3. Ezra Taft Benson, *The Teachings of Ezra Taft Benson* (Salt Lake City: Bookcraft, 1988), p. 71.

4. Story used by permission of the author.

5. Stephen E. Robinson, *Believing Christ* (Salt Lake City: Deseret Book Co., 1992), p. 24. Used by permission.

6. Boyd K. Packer, "Washed Clean," *Ensign,* May 1997, p. 10.

7. Ibid.

10

It is through repentance that the Lord Jesus Christ
can work his healing miracle.
—President Spencer W. Kimball

COME UNTO CHRIST

Several years ago while reading a magazine, I came across a cartoon that pictured a priest seated in a confessional, giving counsel to a parishioner. On the shelves behind the priest and in his lap and hands were many of the self-help books we find in the psychology section of most bookstores. The caption of the cartoon read, "Not to worry, my son. Get off your guilt trip and take the road less traveled. The good book says you're OK. All you need is to pull your own strings, focus on your erroneous zones, take control of your life, and self-actualize yourself so you can achieve your greatest potential . . . and you'll be just fine."[1] On a bottom shelf of the confessional booth rested the Bible—covered with cobwebs.

While at first I found the cartoon to be amusing, I have since come to believe it represents a sobering reality. As a culture we are in the process of forsaking and replacing the teachings of God with the "enticing words of man's wisdom" (1 Corinthians 2:4). Just as the Jews of ancient Israel rejected Jesus Christ as the Messiah, latter-day Israel can lose the light and stumble with the truth because we too are looking beyond the mark (see Jacob 4:14).

Elder Neal A. Maxwell has identified the mark that the Jews

were looking beyond as Jesus Christ.[2] The Jews rejected Jesus as the Messiah because they were expecting their Deliverer to come in power and glory to free them from political bondage. Instead, the Messiah came in a way they did not expect—he came in meekness to deliver them from sin. For centuries many individuals and cultures have either ignored God or rejected the kinds of liberation he has offered and have looked to the philosophies of men for deliverance. The pursuit of pleasure has replaced obedience to God's will as having first priority in our lives. Note the following example from the writings of Elder Boyd K. Packer:

> We live in a day when the adversary stresses on every hand the philosophy of instant gratification. We seem to demand instant everything, including instant solutions to our problems.
>
> We are indoctrinated that somehow we should always be instantly emotionally comfortable. When that is not so, some become anxious—and all too frequently seek relief from counseling, from analysis, and even from medication.
>
> It was meant to be that life would be a challenge. To suffer some anxiety, some depression, some disappointment, even some failure is normal.
>
> Teach our members that if they have a good, miserable day once in a while, or several in a row, to stand steady and face them. Things will straighten out.
>
> There is great purpose in our struggle in life.[3]

Could it be that our culture's obsession with immediate gratification, comfort, ease, and pleasure have caused us to look beyond Christ and have distracted us from the central purposes of our mortal probation? Have we become as the Israelites of old whose lives were centered on eat and drink and play (see Exodus 32:6) and not upon the Savior? Are we brokering our birthrights for a pate of pottage (see Genesis 25:29–34)?

Depression: Sickness, Sin, or Sorrow?

A slogan that has become increasingly popular in the last decade states, "Depression: It's an Illness, Not a Weakness." This expression suggests that earlier ideas about depression being linked to weakness, sin, and lifestyle are old-fashioned and should be abandoned in favor of seeing depression as an illness caused exclusively by a chemical imbalance. For many people who suffer feelings of depression, it is a relief to be told that their problems don't have anything to do with how they are living but need to be understood as a medical condition that can be alleviated through medication. While not all depression is connected to sin an increasing number of people willingly accept the idea that the only responsibility they have in either the cause or the treatment of their "clinical depression" is to take their medication regularly. We need to be ever so careful; for any philosophy that provides a justification for evading moral responsibility (where it is warranted) will only make matters worse.

While I do believe that there are a number of people who are helped by taking antidepressant medications, I also believe others are being misled. In my experience—personally, professionally, and ecclesiastically, feelings of depression or despair are often warning signals that something is amiss in our lives and in need of change. I have no argument with those who believe that people experiencing depression have a chemical imbalance, I am confident that many do. My question is whether or not the chemical imbalance is the cause of depression or the result. If a chemical imbalance is the result (not the cause) of depression and we alleviate the imbalance through medication, we may have left the real reasons for our problems unaddressed and perhaps obscured.

The scriptures contain numerous stories of people who have experienced what could be described as clinical depression. In the Old Testament we find the story of Hannah, who was the mother of the prophet Samuel. Before Hannah gave birth to Samuel, she went through some difficult years. The scriptural account begins by describing two of Hannah's concerns: (1) "And her adversary [her husband's other wife, Peninnah] also provoked her sore, for to make her fret, because the Lord had shut her [Hannah's] womb." (2) "And as he [the Lord] did so [shut her womb] year by year, when she went up to the house of the Lord, so she [Peninnah] provoked her [Hannah]; therefore she wept, and did not eat." (1 Samuel 1:6–7.)

Hannah's situation and symptoms were typical of those of us who experience feelings of depression. She wanted something desperately that she was unable to obtain (in her case, a child), she had a difficult relationship with a family member (Peninnah), she cried often, and had lost her appetite for food.

The response of Hannah's husband is also typical of those who try unsuccessfully to help. Elkanah wanted her to be content with the way things were and not be so concerned about wanting more: "Then said Elkanah her husband to her, Hannah, why weepest thou? and why eatest thou not? and why is thy heart grieved? am not I better to thee than ten sons?" (1 Samuel 1:8; see 1 Nephi 5:2–8 for a better response to a grieving spouse.) After a period of tribulation the Lord blessed Hannah with the knowledge of what she should do. While attending the temple, she made a vow with the Lord that if he were to bless her with a child she would "give him unto the Lord all the days of his life" (1 Samuel 1:11). Of course, the Lord doesn't always bless us with what we want just because we ask for it, but Hannah was exercising faith in what she felt to be the will of the Lord.

At one point in the story, Eli, the presiding High Priest at the temple, feared that Hannah was so full of grief she had been drinking wine and was drunk (see 1 Samuel 1:13). Hannah responded to Eli's concerns by saying: "No, my Lord, I am a woman of a sorrowful spirit: I have drunk neither wine nor strong drink, but have poured out my soul before the Lord. Count not thine handmaid for a daughter of Belial [wickedness]: for out of the abundance of my complaint and grief have I spoken hitherto." (1 Samuel 1:15–16.) Drinking alcohol as a means of dealing with despair was apparently a problem then as it is now, but Hannah knew in whom she could trust. Her despair became an invitation to turn to God.

Eli then admonished and promised Hannah, "Go in peace: and the God of Israel grant thee thy petition that thou hast asked of him" (1 Samuel 1:17). Hannah responded by saying, "Let thine handmaid find grace in thy sight" (1 Samuel 1:18). The text then states that "her countenance was no more sad" (1 Samuel 1:18). It is important to note that Hannah experienced peace before she had given birth or discovered she was pregnant. Hannah's peace came through her faith in the Lord and in the promise of one of his faithful servants.

Elkanah and Hannah returned home and Hannah later gave birth to a baby whom they named Samuel. Consistent with the covenant she had made, after a period of nurturing, Hannah took Samuel to the temple and "lent him to the Lord" (1 Samuel 1:28). Samuel went on to become a great prophet and judge who restored law and order to Israel.

What if Hannah had dealt with her sorrow by turning to wine as Eli had feared? What if she had simply accepted the apparent reality that she would never give birth? My guess is that the miracle of motherhood would have never become a reality for Hannah, but an unclaimed blessing. I also wonder to what extent Hannah's days of tribulation were a part of preparation for her approaching responsibilities as mother to a future prophet of God. It is important for each of us to remember that "after much tribulation come the blessings" (D&C 58:4).

Though Hannah's prayers were eventually answered in the way she had hoped, we must also recognize that the Lord will always fulfill his promises in his own way and in his own time. The scriptures clearly state: "For my thoughts are not your thoughts, neither are your ways my ways, saith the Lord" (Isaiah 55:8). God's will, in many cases, may not be consistent with our own desires, and no matter how many prayers we offer or vows we make, the expected blessing may not come in the way nor at the time we expect (see Malachi 3:14–18).

Life, by eternal design, is meant to be difficult. All of us are going to experience sorrow, even after we are living in the celestial kingdom! The Pearl of Great Price contains an example of God, a perfect being, experiencing sorrow over the wickedness of his children:

> And it came to pass that the God of heaven looked upon the residue of the people, and he wept; and Enoch bore record of it, saying: How is it that the heavens weep, and shed forth their tears as the rain upon the mountains?
>
> And Enoch said unto the Lord: How is it that thou canst weep, seeing thou art holy, and from all eternity to all eternity? . . .
>
> The Lord said unto Enoch: Behold these thy brethren; they are the workmanship of mine own hands, and I gave unto them their knowledge, in the day I created them; and in the Garden of Eden, gave I unto man his agency;
>
> And unto thy brethren have I said, and also given commandment, that they should love one another, and that they should choose me, their Father; but behold, they are without affection, and they hate their own blood. (Moses 7:28–29, 32–33.)

It is interesting to note that in this account, Enoch appears to be surprised by God's expressions of sorrow in response to his children's wickedness. Perhaps Enoch (like many of us), mistakenly equated sorrow and tears with imperfection. The scriptures plainly teach that the emotion of sorrow is a part of the personality of God (see Jacob 5:47; John 11:35).

The Prophet Isaiah taught that sorrow and suffering were a part of the Savior's mortal experience as well: "He is despised and rejected of men; *a man of sorrows,* and *acquainted with grief:* and we hid as it were our faces from him; he was despised, and we esteemed him not. Surely he hath borne our griefs, and carried our sorrows: yet we did esteem him stricken, smitten of God, and afflicted. But he was wounded for our transgressions, he was bruised for our iniquities: the chastisement of our peace was upon him; and with his stripes we are healed." (Isaiah 53:3–5; emphasis added.) Should we be surprised that we too are confronted with sadness and sorrow as a normal and necessary part of the experience of life?

Depression as Sin

The term *depression* is used by many to cover a wide range of emotional experiences. Sadness, sorrow, and sickness can be a normal part of our mortal experience, but feelings of despair are quite different. Notice the distinctions the Apostle Paul makes between being *troubled* and being in *despair:* "We are troubled on every side, yet not distressed; we are perplexed, but not in despair; persecuted, but not forsaken; cast down, but not destroyed" (2 Corinthians 4:8–9). The Hebrew *ya'ash* and Greek *exaporeomai,* both words for despair, are verbs that denote the key element of despair—hopelessness. Moroni taught that "if ye have no hope ye must needs be in despair; and despair cometh because of iniquity" (Moroni 10:22). To have lost hope is to have lost faith—faith in God, in our neighbors, and in ourselves. Moroni points out that despair has its beginnings in iniquity. Remember what President Spencer W. Kimball taught that "the most persistent cause of human suffering, that suffering which causes the deepest pain, is sin."[4] When we sin, we "withdraw [ourselves] from the Spirit of the Lord" (Mosiah 2:36) and are unable to feel his love or the love others have for us. As a young father I was surprised when I would discipline my children by sending them to their rooms, and sometimes one of them would say, "Daddy, you don't love me." Nothing could have been further from the truth, but perhaps my children could not feel my love because, through their disobedience, they had cut themselves off from being able to feel the love that I had for them.

While, as stated earlier, certainly not all feelings of depression come from sin, we would be naive to believe that we can "be restored from sin to happiness" (Alma 41:10). We can't do bad and expect to feel good. As Alma taught his wayward son, Corianton, "wickedness never was happiness" (Alma 41:10). The prophet Mormon provided a similar explanation for the sorrow being experienced by the wicked Nephites: "For their sorrowing was not unto repentance, because of the goodness of God; but it was rather the sorrowing of the damned, because the Lord would not always suffer them to take happiness in sin" (Mormon 2:13).

One of the great dangers in believing that all feelings of depression are caused by something for which we are not responsible, like a chemical imbalance, or the way someone is mistreating us, is that we avoid making necessary changes in the way we are living our lives. Elder Marvin J. Ashton taught: "We often avoid taking action because we tell ourselves that our problem was caused by circumstances or people beyond our control. Therefore we think we can abdicate our responsibility and we find ourselves hoping that other people or a change of conditions will solve our difficulties. Rather, it is our responsibility to repent—to change, and to move forward without delay. 'Do not procrastinate the day of your repentance.' (Alma 34:33.)"[5]

In addition to his invitation to accept personal responsibility for our problems, I have always appreciated Elder Ashton's equating of repentance and change. The Greek word *metanoia* can be interpreted as either of the English words *change* or *repentance*. In other words, the basic idea behind the word *repent* is to change. For some these changes might mean doing less than we are presently doing, for others more. These changes could be as simple as taking better care of our physical bodies or perhaps in not paying as much attention to our physical selves as we have. We might need to do more (or less) in attempting to reconcile with a family member or neighbor (see D&C 42:88; Alma 29:1–4). If we are guilty of a serious sin that could affect our Church membership, we need to see our bishop as soon as possible that he may assist us in making the necessary changes. We shouldn't wait until we are *ready* to repent—waiting will only make things worse.

Repentance Is the Key to the Atonement

The blessed reality behind repentance (or change) is that it is the very key by which we can access the atonement of Jesus Christ. President Kimball once wrote: "The principle of repentance—of rising again whenever we fall, brushing ourselves off, and setting off again on that upward trail—is the basis for our hope. It is through repentance that the Lord Jesus Christ can work his healing miracle, infusing us with strength when we are weak, health when we are sick, hope when we are down-hearted, love when we feel empty, and understanding when we search for truth."[6]

When we sincerely repent, we are meek and teachable and become worthy to feel the influence of the Holy Ghost, which makes it possible for us to experience hope and love: "And the remission of sins bringeth meekness, and lowliness of heart; and because of meekness and lowliness of heart cometh the visitation of the Holy Ghost, which Comforter filleth with hope and perfect love" (Moroni 8:26).

Christine

Repentance is a powerful key that can unlock the door to even the most complicated of problems. When I first met Christine she was a twenty-eight-year-old university student with a multitude of problems. She had been diagnosed as having borderline personality disorder and had been treated with a host of psychiatric medications and psychotherapy for several years. Sadly, it seemed that as the days and months went by, Christine became a threat to herself (suicide) and to her own family. Christine's parents had even begun to make preparations to have her institutionalized in the state mental hospital for an indefinite period of time—they didn't know where else to turn.

As a child Christine had been physically and sexually abused by her brothers. As she grew older she began to experience serious mood swings (which I believe were complicated to some extent by the medications she was taking) and began to cut herself on a regular basis. Even though Christine and her family had spent much time, energy, and money towards her recovery, she didn't seem to be making any progress and even seemed to be getting worse. Miraculously, soon before she was to be institutionalized, things slowly began to change for the better.

While it is difficult to adequately describe all that was a part of Christine's healing, she has identified several essential elements. She first identified that much of the trouble she was experiencing was brought on by what she was doing in the present and not what had happened to her in the past. Christine's bishop shared with her several challenging insights from the scriptures that at first offended her, but in time came to be what started her on the path to being whole. The first comes from the writings of the prophet Lehi to his son Jacob:

> And now, Jacob, I speak unto you: Thou art my first-born in the days of my tribulation in the wilderness. And behold, in thy childhood thou hast suffered afflictions and much sorrow, because of the rudeness of thy brethren.
>
> Nevertheless, Jacob, my first-born in the wilderness, thou knowest the greatness of God; and he shall consecrate thine afflictions for thy gain.
>
> Wherefore, thy soul shall be blessed, and thou shalt dwell safely with thy brother, Nephi; and thy days shall be spent in the service of thy God. Wherefore, I know that thou art redeemed, because of the righteousness of thy Redeemer; for thou hast beheld that in the fulness of time he cometh to bring salvation unto men. (2 Nephi 2:1–3.)

Like Jacob, Christine had grown up suffering afflictions and much sorrow because of the sins of her brethren. She too needed to learn that God could turn her afflictions to her gain. Christine's bishop taught her that while God certainly didn't orchestrate the specifics of Jacob's difficult childhood, nor hers, he allowed the opposition to come about as a part of their mortal probations: "For it must needs be, that there is an opposition in all things. If not so, my first-born in the wilderness, righteousness could not be brought to pass, neither wickedness, neither good nor bad. Wherefore all things must needs be a compound in one." (2 Nephi 2:11.) He also taught her that while counseling and therapy could possibly be of some help to her, it was the Savior to whom she must eventually turn to be healed: "And now, my sons [and daughters], remember, remember that it is upon the rock of our Redeemer, who is Christ, the Son of God, that ye must build your foundation; that when the devil shall send forth his mighty winds, yea, his shafts in the whirlwind, yea, when all his hail and his mighty storm shall beat upon you, it shall have no power over you to drag you down to the gulf of misery and endless wo, because of the rock upon which ye are built, which is a sure foundation, a foundation whereon if men build they cannot fall" (Helaman 5:12).

Christine and her family learned that to truly follow Christ, they must keep his commandments. For different reasons, the following verses from the Doctrine and Covenants had a powerful impact on Christine and her parents:

> My disciples, in days of old, sought occasion against one another and forgave not one another in their hearts; and for this evil they were afflicted and sorely chastened.
>
> Wherefore, I say unto you, that ye ought to forgive one another; for he that forgiveth not his brother his trespasses standeth condemned before the Lord; for there remaineth in him the greater sin.
>
> I, the Lord, will forgive whom I will forgive, but of you it is required to forgive all men.
>
> And ye ought to say in your hearts—let God judge between me and thee, and reward thee according to thy deeds.
>
> And him that repenteth not of his sins, and confesseth them not, ye shall bring before the church, and do with him as the scripture saith unto you, either by commandment or by revelation. (D&C 64:8–12.)

While it is normal for victims of abuse to experience feelings of anger and desires for revenge, these passions will destroy them if they are not dealt with appropriately. That is why the person who is unforgiving is guilty of the greater sin; for, as terrible as the abuse was, it is their own hate that will destroy them and not the abuse. Of course in teaching this doctrine, it is important to explain that for the abuser it is his (or her) abusive behavior that is the greater sin. The Savior warned: "But whoso shall offend one of these little ones which believe in me, it were better for him that a millstone were hanged about his neck, and that he were drowned in the depth of the sea. Woe unto the world because of offences! for it must needs be that offences come; but woe to that man by whom the offence cometh!" (Matthew 18:6–7.)

Christine's parents had been protecting their sons from suffering the consequences of their sins. They thought that if they kept the secret within the family it would be best for all concerned. From Doctrine and Covenants section sixty-four they learned: "And him that repenteth not of his sins, and confesseth them not, ye shall bring before the church" (v. 12). Even though it initially brought some difficult times, disclosure of the specifics of the abuse to the bishop and to legal authorities eventually proved to be a great blessing to Christine, her brothers, and to the family as a whole.

Christine's progress was "precept upon precept; . . . line upon line; here a little, and there a little" (Isaiah 28:13). As odd as it might seem, she began to feel hope as she started to accept responsibility for doing her daily chores. Christine began to shower and brush her teeth regularly and to clean her own room. When it was first discovered that her feelings of depression and self-hate were connected to sexual abuse, Christine's parents felt so sorry for her (and guilty) that they indulged her by not expecting anything from her. They cleaned her room, did her homework, and even brushed her teeth for her!

Christine's healing also included her return to church—first sacrament meeting and then the entire three-hour block. While it was challenging and exhausting for her, she also found great joy in her calling as a Primary teacher. Christine also began to pray and to read the scriptures, searching for light and knowledge. Several months into her study of the standard works, Christine found a verse in the New Testament she believed was just for her: "There is nothing from without [outside] a man, that entering into him can defile him: but the things which come out of him, those are they that defile the man" (Mark 7:15). This verse led Christine to understand that not only must she forgive her brothers, she must also avoid defiling herself by using their sins against her as justification for her sins against them. She came to realize that being raped and abused didn't take her virtue; her virtue was something only she could give up.

Christine began to examine her behavior towards her brothers for any evidence of sin she had committed against them. During the months that followed, Christine realized that she had fabricated some of the story about the abuse; she had borne "false witness" (Exodus 20:16) against her brothers. To Christine's credit, with the help of her bishop, she met with her brothers and asked them to forgive her for making an already horrible situation worse.

It has been a joy to watch Christine progress. She has married and she and her husband are rearing their three little girls. She struggles with the problems of life and at times even finds herself in despair over what happened in the past, but Christine can say with Nephi, "I know in whom I have trusted. My God hath been my support." (2 Nephi 4:19–20.)

There were several things that I observed and learned as I was privileged to go through this experience as Christine's friend and teacher. Even though she was extremely confused and fearful about what was happening to her in the present, what had happened to her in her past, and who she would become in the future, she continued to have access to her divine identity as a daughter of God with a divine past and potential.

Amidst the darkness of Christine's confused state, she continued to have access to the truth through her conscience—a very personal sense of who she really was, and what God would have her do to find the wholeness she was seeking.

Christine once shared with me how she had noticed that her periods of anger and depression usually followed the times when she had been invited, either by the Spirit or by someone else, to improve her life in some way. Often these invitations included doing something for someone else. Even though she had access to what she needed to be doing through her conscience, she eclipsed herself from it with rationalizations and negative, hateful emotions. The adversary, and some of his colleagues, had tricked her into believing that the abuse she had suffered had made it impossible for her to move forward.

As Christine began to understand that her problems were in the present (what she was doing, not in what had been done to her), she began to feel hope. She came to understand that the answers to her problems were contained in the gospel of Jesus Christ, specifically in the doctrine of the Atonement. She came to realize that no one could save her except the Savior—as with all of us, without the Atonement she would perish.

Conclusion

The Savior taught that "the key of knowledge [is the] fullness of the scriptures" (JST, Luke 11:53). The restoration of the fulness of the scriptures through the Prophet Joseph Smith provides the means by which each of us can learn to understand ourselves, the world around us and the heavens beyond. It is my belief and experience that all of the personal, marital, and family problems we face can be alleviated by understanding and living the gospel of Jesus Christ. The scriptures and the words of our living prophets provide a doctrinal framework that enables us to understand the great plan of happiness which has been given to us by a loving Heavenly Father. Elder Neal A. Maxwell has stated: "So vital is this framework that if one stays or strays outside it, he risks provinciality and misery. In fact, most human misery represents ignorance of or noncompliance with the plan. A cessation of such mortal suffering will not come without compliance to it."[7]

Central to this plan of redemption is the atonement of Jesus Christ. Elder Maxwell explained further: "In addition to bearing our sins—the required essence of the Atonement—the 'how' of which we certainly do not understand, Jesus is further described as having come to know our sicknesses, griefs, pains, and infirmities as well. Another 'how' we cannot comprehend! (See Isaiah 53:4; Matthew 8:17; Mosiah 14:4; Alma 7:11–12.) Jesus thus not only satisfied the requirements of divine justice but also, particularly in His Gethsemane and Calvary ordeals, demonstrated and perfected His capacity to succor His people and His empathy for them."[8]

Inasmuch as we access the power of the Atonement through repentance, the first question we need to ask ourselves when facing the problems of life is, "Do I understand the gospel and am I living in harmony with all of God's laws?" President Ezra Taft Benson teaches us this truth in the following:

> In the Book of Mormon we read that "despair cometh because of iniquity." (Moroni 10:22.) . . . Sin pulls a man down into despondency and despair. While a man may take some temporary pleasure in sin, the end result is unhappiness. "Wickedness never was happiness." (Alma 41:10.) Sin creates disharmony with God and is depressing to the spirit. Therefore, a man would do well to examine himself to see that he is in harmony with all of God's laws. Every law kept brings a particular blessing. Every law broken brings a particular blight. Those who are heavy-laden with despair should come unto the Lord, for his yoke is easy and his burden is light. (See Matthew 11:28–30.)"[9]

We are often too quick to seek explanations outside of our own sins for the problems that we face. Many of us are quick to blame our problems on another, or upon circumstances which we deem beyond our control. We feel that if the other person would change or if our circumstances would change that our problems would be solved. The truth is that we need to make sure we are following the Lord's plan in doing "all we can do" (2 Nephi 25:23) to alleviate the problems we are facing. Otherwise, we may miss the very solution which we are seeking.

In addition to blaming someone or something for our problems, many of us expect someone else (friend, bishop, therapist, etc.) or something else (medication, therapy, book, seminar, etc.) to be the solution to our problems. By seeking for answers from these sources first, we deny ourselves of a marvelous opportunity for spiritual growth and maturity. Elder Boyd K. Packer has written, "We [the Brethren] have become very anxious over the amount of counseling that we seem to need in the Church. Our members are becoming dependent. . . . If we are not careful, we can lose the power of individual revelation."[10]

Our Heavenly Father is anxious to bless us with his love and wisdom. He has promised that he will never abandon us. Elder George Q. Cannon stated:

You may be as humble and as obscure as it is possible for a human being to be; but I say to you God will never forget the covenant that he has made with you, and that you have made with Him. . . . Some people seem to forget the promises which God has made, and they become discouraged and think they are forgotten by God. I tell you that God is watching over all of you. . . . He will hear our prayers in hours of despair and darkness, when it would seem as though we were friendless, if we go to Him and call upon Him. He is a God near at hand, and not afar off. He will help us and open our way before us. And we should exercise faith in Him. That is the great principle that we should hang on to and cultivate—faith in God and in His ability and willingness to grant unto us the righteous desires of our hearts. We forget this too often. We go along as though we had no friend in the heavens. We should dismiss such thoughts from our hearts, and live so near unto the Lord that He will give unto us continually His Holy Spirit, filling our hearts with joy and peace. . . . This is the spirit that we should all seek for, and not give way to gloomy feelings, or to murmuring. If men do not suit you, make God your friend. He says, "Cursed is he that putteth his trust in man, or maketh flesh his arm." The man that trusts in his fellow man is likely to be deceived. Men will fail; husbands will fail; wives will fail; children will fail; parents will fail; but God never fails. He never grows cold, or indifferent. He is always the same unchangeable being, and His promises can be relied upon to the very uttermost. . . . He will be with us in the deep water. He will be with us in the fiery furnace. He will be with us under all circumstances, if we serve Him.[11]

Throughout this book I have attempted to provide a variety of examples from the lives of men and women who found the answers they were seeking by petitioning God and living by his word in spite of the magnitude of the challenges they were facing. Many will argue the point that the gospel truths are too simplistic to address the complex problems of our day. As I described in the introduction to this book, it is from Nephi's answer to this objection, I have taken the title of this book: "He sent fiery flying serpents among them; and after they were bitten he prepared a way that they might be healed; and the labor which they had to perform was to look; and because of *the simpleness of the way,* or the easiness of it, there were many who perished" (1 Nephi 17:41; emphasis added).

While the scriptures do not promise great temporal prosperity, prestige, or freedom from the problems of the world, they do contain promises of peace in the midst of adversity if we live the simple principles taught therein. The Savior taught: "Peace I leave with you, my peace I give unto you: not as the world giveth, give I unto you. Let not your heart be troubled, neither let it be afraid." (John 14:27.)

We are children of a Heavenly Father who loves us. He has given us a plan, even the great plan of the Eternal God, that we may have joy in this life and eternal life in the world to come.

Therefore, cheer up your hearts, and remember that ye are free to act for yourselves—to choose the way of everlasting death or the way of eternal life.

Wherefore, my beloved brethren, reconcile yourselves to the will of God, and not to the will of the devil and the flesh; and remember, after ye are reconciled unto God, that it is only in and through the grace of God that ye are saved.

Wherefore, may God raise you from death by the power of the resurrection, and also from everlasting death by the power of the atonement, that ye may be received into the eternal kingdom of God, that ye may praise him through grace divine. Amen. (2 Nephi 10:23–25.)

NOTES

1. In *His,* December 1984, p. 12.
2. See Neal A. Maxwell, "'Jesus of Nazareth, Savior and King'," *Ensign,* May 196, p. 26.
3. Boyd K. Packer, *That All May Be Edified* (Salt Lake City: Bookcraft, 1982), p. 94.
4. Spencer W. Kimball, *The Teachings of Spencer W. Kimball,* ed. Edward L. Kimball (Salt Lake City: Bookcraft, 1982), p. 155.
5. Marvin J. Ashton, "Straightway," *Ensign,* May 1983, p. 32.
6. Kimball, *The Teachings of Spencer W. Kimball,* p. 106.
7. Neal A. Maxwell, "The Great Plan of the Eternal God," *Ensign,* May 1984, p. 21.
8. Neal A. Maxwell, *"Not My Will, But Thine"* (Salt Lake City: Bookcraft, 1988), p. 51.
9. Ezra Taft Benson, "Do Not Despair," *Ensign,* October 1986, p. 2.
10. Boyd K. Packer, "Solving Emotional Problems in the Lord's Own Way," *Ensign,* May 1978, p. 92.
11. George Q. Cannon, "Need for Prophets," in *Collected Discourses,* vol. 2, (Burbank, California: B.H.S. Publishing, 1988), pp. 333–34.

INDEX